Berkeley's Analysis of Perception

PETER LANG
New York · San Francisco · Bern
Frankfurt am Main · Paris · London

George J. Stack

Berkeley's Analysis of Perception

PETER LANG
New York · San Francisco · Bern
Frankfurt am Main · Paris · London

Library of Congress Cataloging-in-Publication Data

Stack, George J.
Berkeley's analysis of perception / George J. Stack.
p. cm.
Reprint. Originally published: The Hague : Mouton, 1970.
Includes bibliographical references.
1. Berkeley, George, 1685-1753 – Contributions in concept of perception. 2. Perception (Philosophy) – History – 18th century.
I. Title.
B1349.P4S7 1991 121'.3 – dc20 90-23674
ISBN 0-8204-1528-6 CIP

CIP-Titelaufnahme der Deutschen Bibliothek

George J. Stack:
Berkeley's analysis of perception / George J. Stack. – New York; Bern; Frankfurt am Main; Paris: Lang, 1991
ISBN 0-8204-1528-6

The paper in this book meets the guidelines for permanence and durability of the Committee on Production Guidelines for Book Longevity of the Council on Library Resources.

Printed in the United States of America.

Contents

Introduction

The most fundamental aim of this enquiry will be to provide a critical analysis of, and re-examination of, Berkeley's description of the process of perception and to analyze the various aspects of his theory of perception. In addition, attention will be focused upon the question of the relationship between Berkeley's perceptual theory and the contemporary phenomenalistic analysis of perception. One basic and underlying assumption of this investigation will be that there is a distinct continuity and development in Berkeley's thought which can be traced through all of his reflective analyses of the problem of perception.

Berkeley's typical approach to a philosophical question is a polemical one. The materials which the youthful Berkeley concerned himself with in his notebook, the *Commonplace Book*, indicated not only the philosophical puzzles which interested him at the time, but illustrated the targets against which he would later direct his philosophical fire. The basic intentions which Berkeley expressed in his notebook were the following: to attack the general tendency towards skepticism which was epitomized by Pierre Bayle's *Dictionnaire historique et critique* and which, in Berkeley's eyes, threatened to undermine Christian morality and the Christian *Weltanschauung*; to war against the notion of Malbranche that man can have access to the divine mind or ideas; to criticize Newton's notion that space is the *sensorium Dei* (the divine sensorium in which God is present through his intellect and will as the guide of the events of the natural world) and to point out the difficulties into which the hypostatization of the Newtonian scientific concepts can lead; to undermine Locke's conception of abstract ideas and launch an attack against the representational theory of perception in general; to defend a notion which may be thought of as a fundamental sentiment of his thought, that "nothing properly but persons, i.e. conscious things, do exist", against those who maintained that the basic existent was material substance; and, finally, to launch a counterattack against skeptics and materialists by forging the weapon of immaterialism.

The first stage of what A. A. Luce has recently called Berkeley's "dialectic of immaterialism" was the critical analysis of the traditional theories of vision of those whom Berkeley referred to as the "optic writers" and the constructive formulation of a "new theory of vision" which ultimately led to the development of the so-called "doctrine of immaterialism". In his early work, *Essay towards a New Theory of Vision*, Berkeley introduces the fundamental themes which pervade his analyses of perception – the concept of IDEA which was introduced to refer to the elementary data of sense-experience, the conception of the heterogeneity of the "ideas" of sight and touch, the notion of suggestion which involved the application of associationist psychology to the study of perception, the distinction between immediate and mediate perception, the conception of *minima sensibilia*, and the emphasis upon the mind-dependent status of "ideas" of sight or visual "sense-data". In the examination of Berkeley's theory of vision an attempt will be made to show that perception, for Berkeley, is the apprehension of phenomenal appearances alone, that – in Berkeley's terminology – the ideas of sight do not "represent" anything which is outside or "without the mind". It will be assumed, in the examination of the new theory of vision, that the ostensible "realism" in regard to tactile sense-impressions is merely a concession which Berkeley made to philosophical views held at the time of the writing of the *Essay towards a New Theory of Vision*, and can in no way be thought to be his considered opinion. It will be seen that, in this early work, there are strong phenomenalistic elements in his analysis of visual perception which will be emphasized later in his *Principles of Human Knowledge* and in the *Three Dialogues between Hylas and Philonous*. In these later works Berkeley argues in defense of the mind-dependent nature of ALL "ideas of sense" or "sense-data" and the view that perception involves the apprehension of a "system of appearances" which is caused by the activity of a transphenomenal being, God.

In the specific analysis of Berkeley's statements about the nature of the perceptual process, it will be seen that perception is described, despite occasional protests to the contrary, as a passive process. The elementary data of sense-experience are said to be "imprinted" on our senses, and they are "given" to a perceiver. In Berkeley's account of sense-perception it will be seen that the perceiver is passively receptive to phenomena. In the final analysis, it may be said that, for Berkeley, action is ineluctably related to the activity of "volition". Despite Berkeley's denials, it will be shown that there is in his description of perception a clear tendency to conceive of perception as primarily a passive process. The implications of such an interpretation of Berkeley are significant insofar as they affect our understanding of the phenomenalistic aspects of his analysis of perception.

Throughout this examination of Berkeley's discussion of perception an attempt will be made to point out some of the internal difficulties which such a discussion seems to encounter. Thus, for example, it will be shown that Berkeley's theory of perception incorporates distinct aspects of the representational theory of perception which he had attacked and that the mode of representationalism which is a real, if implicit, aspect of his analysis of perception was, in a sense, a "product" of his interpretation of the perceptual process in general. In addition, the significant role which imagination plays in Berkeley's thought will be pointed out, especially in relation to the rudimentary form of "constructionism" which, it is believed, is present in his description of the nature of perception.

The principal aim of this investigation, aside from a critical examination of the detailed structure of Berkeley's theory of perception, will be to show that Berkeley is not only a species of phenomenalist, but the prototype of the phenomenalist. Perception, it will be argued, is, for Berkeley, the apprehension of a multiplicity of phenomenal data of sense. What may be called the "phenomenal objects" of sense-perception have a relative and dependent mode of "existence" which is contrasted with the absolute existence of "things" which are, according to Berkeley, objects of the divine mind. This metaphysical characteristic of Berkeley's thought is one which must be examined if a distortion of his analysis of perception is to be avoided.

In order to determine the conceptual structure of Berkeley's study of the problem of perception it will be necessary to deal with the relationship between his description of perception and the contemporary forms of phenomenalistic theories of perception. Although it will be maintained that there are obvious inchoate anticipations of what has come to be called linguistic phenomenalism in Berkeley's thought, it will be argued that Berkeley's metaphysics and his obvious retention of factual reference in his analysis of perception estrange him from this mode of phenomenalism. The transformations of the formulations of phenomenalistic analyses of perception will be traced primarily in relation to the way in which Berkeley approached such an interpretation of the nature of the perceptual process.

This analysis of the fundamental elements of Berkeley's discussion of perception will proceed in the following way: in Chapter I an attempt will be made to trace the development of the conception of "immaterialism" through an examination of Berkeley's theory of vision and to indicate some of the basic problems which this theory seems to encounter; in Chapter II attempts will be made to defend Berkeley against some of the various criticisms which have been brought against his conception of the mind-dependent nature of the elementary sensory data, to delineate the process which Berkeley described as "spiritual causation", to examine the problem of identity, and to draw out the implications of Berkeley's distinction between the phenomena apprehended by finite minds and the "ideas" known by the divine mind; in Chapter III a critical examination of the usage of the term "idea" will be presented and interrelated with an account of the concept of a "sensible object" or thing; and, finally, Chapter IV will be concerned with a discussion of the relationship between Berkeley's perceptual analysis and the basic forms of contemporary phenomenalism.

The thread which runs through the various analyses of perception in the writings of Berkeley will be traced from his early delineation of the nature of visual sense-perception in his *Essay towards a New Theory of Vision* to the occasional but revealing comments which are made concerning perception in the *Siris*. Although it has been necessary to consider tangentially Berkeley's conception of God, this inquiry is not primarily concerned with the theological problems with which Berkeley concerns himself in, for example, the *Alciphron*. Specific emphasis has been placed upon those aspects of Berkeley's writings which deal, either directly or indirectly, with the various problems of perception. An attempt has been made to avoid unnecessary digressions from this central focus of attention. Although there has been a vast amount of work done in the problem of perception in recent years, it is believed that the examination of Berkeley's discussion of perception is a fruitful enterprise since so much work in the study of sense-perception is either derived from Berkeley's original work or is in reaction to the paradoxes into which, it is thought, the form in which he stated his analysis of perception have led him and other philosophers who have been influenced by his work. In addition, the obvious relationship which exists between Berkeley's formulations of his interpretation of perception and the formulations of phenomenalists makes an analysis of the precise details of that relationship relevant to some of the contemporary discussions of the problems of perception.

Although Berkeley had, in his early notebook, written a memorandum to himself reminding him to recall men to common sense and to abandon metaphysics, he can hardly be said to have been faithful to his own advice. Recent studies of Berkeley's thought have endeavored to point out that if Berkeley's writings could be purified of some unfortunate modes of expression, then he could be said have been a precursor of the linguistic approach to philosophical problems. There is, no doubt, some evidence for this view. But the attempt to avoid a discussion of his metaphysical beliefs or to treat them lightly has led, it is believed, to serious misinterpretations of his thought. The notions that there is design in the universe, that there is a divine providence which governs the happenings in the temporal world, that a divine being is the cause of our sense-impressions are views which Berkeley never abandoned. He did not, by any means, banish metaphysics. Nor, on the other hand, can he be said to be a champion of common sense. The description of perception which he provided may, indeed, allow us to talk about sensible objects; but the terminology he used, the sophisticated arguments he presented in defense of the mind-dependent status of what he called "ideas of sense", remove him from the realm of common sense. It is believed that some traditional interpretations of Berkeley's analysis of perception as a form of common sense realism are mistaken. A detailed examination of the fundamental structure of his theory of perception will reveal a clear commitment to a fundamentally phenomenalistic analysis of perception. If the implications of his description of the perceptual process are drawn out and are examined in the various contexts in which he specifically deals with the problem of perception, it will be seen that, in the final analysis, the view that Berkeley has presented a form of common sense realism is untenable, that his mode of interpreting the process of perception is more closely allied with that of phenomenalism or, if the anachronism would be permitted, phenomenological descriptions of perception as it is immediately experienced.

I

Berkeley's Analysis of Perception: The New Theory of Vision

> What appears is a vision of the unseen.
> Anaxagoras, Fragment 21a

The problem of perception is the central *leitmotiv* of Berkeley's writings. From the skeptical and rudimentary inquiries of his notebook, the *Commonplace Book*, to the Neo-Platonic repudiation of the realm of sense-perception in the *Siris*, the specter of the question of perception haunts his thought. Berkeley's early *Essay towards a New Theory of Vision* indicates (1) his obvious preoccupation with the problem of perception and (2) the path by which he was led to his positive doctrine of immaterialism and his critique of the absolute existence of material substance. For these reasons this essay will be the starting point for this investigation.

Though it is obvious that the problem of perception did not spring, like Zeus' Athena, from the head of Berkeley, it is equally obvious that the historical approach to Berkeley's investigation of perception and knowledge has been carried out too often and too well to bear repetition here. Hence, this inquiry will plunge *in medias res*, grappling with the problem of perception as Berkeley understands it, avoiding, as far as possible, the temptation to view Berkeley's thought through the telescopes of the past or the microscopes of the present.

Berkeley announces that his intention in his *Essay towards a New Theory of Vision* is to demonstrate the way in which we perceive through vision the distance, magnitude and situation of objects. In addition, he intends to examine the differences between "ideas" of sight and "ideas" of touch, to determine whether there is any idea common to both senses.[1] It is interesting to note that Berkeley focuses his attention on visual and tactile perception with the exception of passing references to aural perception. This certainly is not surprising since the dominant focus of attention in perception has been placed – from Plato and Aristotle to the present – upon visual and tactile perception. One manifestation of this focus of interest is the numerous metaphors – pandemic in philosophical writings – related to cognition, but obviously derived from the language of visual and tactile sense-perception. Thus, for example, we commonly speak of someone "seeing" (i.e., understanding) the solution of a problem. Descartes' notion of "clear" ideas is obviously derived from the language of visual perception. In Sanskrit the word for knowledge, *vidya*, is derived from the word, *vid*, "to see". The word "theory" is derived from the Greek word *theorein*, "to look at", "to behold". The German word *Begriff* ("concept") betrays its indebtedness to the sensation of touch (*Griff* = "grip", "grasp"). In English when we say that we understand or *comprehend* something, we metaphorically mean that we "catch hold of", or "seize" (*prehendere*) something. The Italian word *capire* may mean either "to see" or "to understand". Though many other illustrations could be provided, it would be superfluous reiteration of the obvious relationship between the language of visual and tactile perception and the language of thought. Berkeley's emphasis upon the "ideas" of sight and touch is one which pervades the philosophical literature on perception.

A. The New Theory of Vision

The general purpose of Berkeley's *Essay towards a New Theory of Vision* is (a) to criticize current theories concerning the perception of distance and magnitude put forward by men whom Berkeley variously calls the "optic writers" or "mathematicians"; (b) to delineate his own theory of vision and to emphasize the distinction between ideas of sight and ideas of touch. Though Berkeley's criticism of the views of the "optic writers" might seem, on the surface, the least interesting aspect of his theory of vision, a brief review of that criticism is necessary in order to illuminate the paths by which Berkeley arrived at his formulation of a theory of vision.

In the theories of optics of his contemporaries (Berkeley seems to have in mind W. Molyneux's *Treatise of Dioptrics* and Isaac Barrow's *Optical Lectures*) it was argued that we "judge" distance or, to use Berkeley's term, "outness" by a kind of geometrical calculation. Thus, for example, the two optic axes which concur at an object form an angle by means of which – whether the angle be of a greater or lesser degree – the object is perceived to be closer to, or farther away from, the observer.[2]

Berkeley raises three essential objections against the views of the optics writers. One premise of his initial objection is rather interesting because of the way in which it illustrates the ambiguity of Berkeley's conception of perception. This premise is that the mind, when it perceives any idea not immediately and not in itself, must perceive such an idea by means of another idea. The illustration Berkeley provides in order to support this belief is revealing. He claims that we can "see shame or fear in the looks of a man" simply by means of the perception of the change of color of his countenance.[3]

Now it is obvious that we do not "see" shame or fear, but that we may be said to infer the presence of such emotional states in others from what we actually see. We simply do not perceive another's passions by sight. In addition, the implicit equation of passions "in the mind" of others with ideas would seem to involve Berkeley in some difficulty. How can passions "in the mind" of another person be termed ideas? The emotional states of another are not ideas "in my mind" nor are they MY sensations. Despite the apparent difficulties in which Berkeley seems to involve himself at this point in his discussion of visual perception – difficulties which will be examined in detail elsewhere – he had, nevertheless, a valid point to make. Simply, that the formation of a judgment on any particular occasion must be guided by something of which we are actually aware of on that occasion. Judgment of distance, for example, must be arrived at on the basis of data or "visual cues" which are acquired in the process of perception.

The optical writers, as we have seen, assert that we judge distance through the perception of angles of convergence of light rays or the angles of intersection of the optic axes. Though such a theory of the perception of distance may be fruitful in optical studies, it is obvious that a person untrained in optics does not, in fact, use such information in judging distance. It is equally obvious that we simply do not perceive lines from our eyes converging upon an object or lines from an object converging upon each eye. Berkeley argues that, since we do not actually see such lines and angles which the optic writers speak of, we cannot be said to judge distance by means of them. For, as Berkeley puts it, we cannot mediately perceive distances on the basis of what is imperceptible. "No idea which is not itself perceived can be . . . the means of perceiving any other idea."[4] Berkeley's second objection against the views of the "mathematicians" is that the angles and lines they speak of have no real existence in nature and are simply hypothetical constructs or *entia rationis* which are used in optical studies in order that such studies might be presented in precise geometrical terms. Another way to express this objection would be to say that the optic writers are attempting to translate a qualitative process into quantitive terms. This objection of Berkeley's would seem to be rather weak. For, in all probability, the optical writers themselves would not claim that the lines and angles they describe have any real existence in nature. But, nevertheless, they would still probably insist that it is by means of the theoretical notions they describe that we truly judge distance.

Berkeley's third reason for objecting to the views of the optical theoreticians is that even if the real existence of optical angles is granted and even if it is admitted that such angles are perceived, such notions would be insufficient to explain the phenomenon of distance. At this point in his discussion Berkeley proceeds to present his own theory of vision, focusing his attention upon the problem of the visual perception of distance. Against the optic writers Berkeley basically argued that the concepts used by them are indeed useful in computation, but that the "mind" does not judge distances by means of them. Judgment of distances is dependent upon certain visual and nonvisual (kinesthetic) "cues" which are the essential experiential data which determine such judgment.

Beginning with the assertion which he will iterate again and again, Berkeley affirms that we do not perceive distance directly or immediately, but that distance is "suggested" to the mind by some other idea which is apprehended in the act of visual perception. There are, he insists, ideas or sensations which accompany vision with which ideas of distance are joined and by which such ideas (of distance) are "suggested" to the mind. The introduction of the term suggestion is an attempt to explain the phenomenon of the customary association of ideas which is related to Berkeley's theory of signs. This "doctrine" of suggestion is one of the central themes which pervades Berkeley's philosophy.

At any rate, Berkeley contends that in judging distance we sometimes perceive the muscular strain which is required in order to see clearly an object which approaches us or recedes from us. That is, we are aware of the muscular strain required in the process of accommodation – the contraction of pupils and the convergence of the eyes which is accomplished by the contraction and relaxation of the ciliary muscle. This sensation is not, however, a visual sensation, but a tactile sensation.[5] There would seem to be one simple objection which could be made against this assertion. We may ask whether, in fact, we are actually aware of having the sensation in question. Does not the process of accommodation merely become an habitual reaction (like the contraction of the iris in response to the stimulus of light) which is both involuntary and unconscious? It is interesting to note, anyway, that the apparently innocuous analogy which Berkeley offers in support of the above assertion illustrates a rather fundamental difficulty in Berkeley's theory. For, he claims that the sensations accompanying the change in the disposition of the eyes "suggest" the idea of distance which is customarily connected with that sensation. The analogy he offers is the following: the above process is similar to the process by which a certain sound, say, a whistle, immediately "suggests" to the understanding that which custom has united with it (say, a train). Now, it is obvious that the two conditions are not actually similar. In the one case, a sensation is perceived (e.g., a sound) and something other than this sensation is inferred by an act of the UNDERSTANDING. In the other case, there are two elements which are perceived. (1) The sensation of muscular strain (the tactile sensation) and (2) the visual perception of an "object" which, we may suppose, appears in space. Again, the percipient is said to perceive the "idea" of distance mediately on the basis of what is perceived immediately. But in the analogy which Berkeley puts forward, we are concerned not with perception primarily, but with an act of the understanding. That is to say, with an inference.

It would appear that Berkeley intends to demonstrate that we do perceive the idea of distance (if not immediately, at least mediately) and not that we infer the idea of distance from what we do perceive. We arrive at the idea of distance not by an act of the understanding, but by the process of perception. Berkeley cannot mean to suggest that the idea of distance is an *ens rationis* since he repeatedly insists that such an idea arises out of perception and is not simply a concept "produced" by the understanding. Two major difficulties, at any rate, are exposed in this discussion: (1) Berkeley's tendency to vacillate between conceiving of inference as a function of perception or of the understanding; (2) the notorious ambiguity of the term "idea" in Berkeley's writings. Berkeley's second illustration of the way in which we perceive distance refers to the fact that objects often appear to be "out of focus". That is, " . . . the nearer it is brought the more confused appearance it makes".[6] Since this phenomenon is found to be constant, Berkeley argues, an habitual connection is formed in consciousness between the degrees of confusion (in the appearance of an object) and distance. The greater the confusion of the appearance of an object, the lesser the distance and the lesser the confusion of the appearance the greater the distance of the object. Although this illustration would seem to carry more weight in support of

Berkeley's position than the first illustration, it could be argued that the appearance of distant objects would also seem to be "out of focus" and to present a "confused appearance". Nevertheless, it must be admitted that there seems to be a distinct phenomenological difference between the perception of a "distant" object — no matter how confused such an appearance may be — and the perception of an object which is extremely close to our eyes.

Berkeley's third illustration offered in support of his position seems to be intimately related to his first assertion. He claims that we can prevent the appearance of an object from becoming more confused by "straining the eye". In such an instance, this sensation aids the mind to judge the distance of an object. The greater the straining of the eyes, the closer an object is judged to be to the perceiver.

It is contended by Berkeley that the orthodox writers on optics (of his day) are wrong in their account of the way in which we perceive distance. To be sure, he is willing to admit that optics aids us in the measurement of distance or in the understanding of the scientific description of the geometric structure of visual perception. But there is a distinct difference, Berkeley argues, between the measurement or calculation of distance and the judging or estimation of distance. What aids us in the concrete act of judging distance is the appearance of things or objects, the customary assumptions and beliefs we have about such appearances and, in some instances, the sensations which we are aware of on the occasion of perceiving distance (e.g., the tactile sensations discussed above). There is, Berkeley insists, an habitual or customary connection (not, however, a necessary connection) between the visual and tactile cues apprehended in sense-perception and the idea of distance. Since there is no necessary connection between the cues by which we judge distance and the idea of distance *per se*, we are dependent upon experience (and the learning derived from experience) for the estimates we make of the apparent distance of objects. After his analysis of the judgment of distance Berkeley proceeds to examine the question of the perception of the situation of objects.

B. The Situation of Objects

A brief examination of Berkeley's discussion of the "situation" of objects is necessary because it is by means of this inquiry that a transition is made to an analysis of the difference between the ideas of sight and the ideas of touch. It had been observed that if we pass light through a lens which resembles the human eye and project the resulting image upon a screen behind it, the pattern formed on the screen will be upside down. Thus, if the source of light has a pyramid shape when it is standing on its base, the shape which is projected on the screen will be that of a pyramid which is standing on its apex. If, to use another example, we take the figure of a tree as the source from which light is reflected into the eye, the resulting pattern formed on the retina will have the same shape, but the image will be inverted. How is it possible, then, that the tree is seen upright and not in an inverted position? It was believed by the optic writers that the rays of light which are emitted or reflected from an object cross each other in the eye. Thus, since we perceive an impulse of a ray of light on the upper portion of the eye, we imagine that this ray emanates in a straight line from the lower part of the object. Conversely, we believe that the impulse which we perceive as "touching" the lower part of the eye emanates (in a straight line) from the upper portion of the object. The analogy used to illustrate this phenomenon – an analogy, incidentally, apparently derived from Descartes' work on Dioptrices[7] – is the following: we may imagine that an object is felt by the use of two sticks which are crossed. The stick held in the upper hand would be touching the lower part of the object and the stick held in the lower hand would be touching the upper part of it. This account of the matter under discussion is objected to by Berkeley on the ground that it presupposes that, in our ordinary perception, we are aware of, or cognizant of, sophisticated optical theories and that we are constantly involved in the process of correcting our ordinary sense-impressions. That is, the implication of the discussion of the optical theories is that we are continually correcting the immediate impression that an object appears to the eye as an inverted image by our knowledge of optics.

The entire discussion in which Berkeley engages himself at this point is actually rather puzzling. Recently, a number of interpretations of Berkeley's analysis of the "knot about inverted images" have been examined by E. J. Furlong.[8] D. M. Armstrong's interpretation of Berkeley's treatment of the "inverted image" involves the assertion that Berkeley did hold that retinal images are immediate objects of sight. Armstrong makes this assertion on the basis of the assumption that Berkeley could not offer the simple solution to the "knot about inverted images" – that the ostensible "pictures" on the retina are not pictures at all – because his analysis of distance more or less forced him to accept the view that we do in fact see our own retinas or the pictures "painted" on them. C. M. Turbayne claims, on the other hand, that Berkeley adopted the view that retinal images are immediate objects of sight purely for dialectical purposes. Though it would seem that Berkeley does not offer the simple solution to this "knot" in the *Essay towards a New Theory of Vision*, i.e., that we do not, in fact, see these images, there is evidence (from the *Commonplace Book* and the *Theory of Vision Vindicated and Explained*) that he was quite aware of such a solution. It would appear that in adopting the notion that we see the inverted images "painted" on our retinas Berkeley was, as Turbayne claims, merely accepting the view of his opponents for dialectical purposes. In effect, however, Berkeley attempted to adopt the position that we do not perceive an erect appearance of an object but we do "see" images on the retina which are not inverted. Berkeley adopts the view that the "pictures" on the retina are the immediate objects of sight and are hence mind-dependent or are "in the mind". It is believed that Berkeley adopted the above views in the *Essay towards a New Theory of Vision* for the following reasons: (a) ostensibly to adopt his opponents' views in order to show later the inadequacy of such views and (b) to capitalize, as it were, on the notion that the images on the retina are (as the immediate objects of sight) "in the mind" and hence to elicit support for his notion that ideas of sight are not "external" to the perceiver. The belief that Berkeley has adopted a position for dialectical purposes is supported by his ostensible conclusion at the end of the *Essay towards a New Theory of Vision* that the objects of touch are "outside" the mind. This conclusion is obviously incompatible with his position in the *Principles* and indicates the way in which he was able to adopt viewpoints foreign to his essential position for dialectical reasons. If our second assumption is correct, it may be that Berkeley began to see that he did not need to suppose that we see pictures on the retina in order to emphasize the mind-dependent "status" of the objects of vision. Since it appears from the *Commonplace Book* that Berkeley was aware of the simple solution to the "knot about inverted images", i.e. that we do not, in fact, see such pictures on the retina, Turbayne's interpretation of Berkeley's treatment of this question seems quite plausible.

At any rate, Berkeley argues that the official theory of the optical writers contains another difficulty. That is, that the terms "erect" and "inverted" do not, in any way, have any actual reference to visual sense-data at all; rather, they are terms which may be more accurately referred to the sense of touch. It is, Berkeley asserts, by reference to the "tangible earth" that we determine position or situation. Berkeley argues that we actually cannot assert that things appear to be situated in any other way than in the way in which they are actually situated. There is, he insists, no real relation between objects or things which we "see" and "tangible" objects as they actually are. This objection which Berkeley offers is actually anticipatory since it depends upon the conclusions he reaches in his intricate discussion of the distinction between visual and tactile sense-data.

Before we enter into a discussion of this distinction, it may be of interest to consider a criticism of Berkeley's discussion of the retinal image proffered by D. M. Armstrong. Armstrong avers[9] that Berkeley is prevented from distinguishing between the visible retinal image and the immediate objects of sight simply because this kind of distinction would undermine his fundamental premiss. That is, that distance is not immediately perceived since, as Berkeley puts it,

> . . . distance being a line directed end-wise to the eye, it projects only one point in the fund of the eye, which point remains invariably the same, whether the distance be longer or shorter.[10]

This argument, Armstrong insists, is valid only if we consider that the immediate object of sight is actually the fund of the eye. Now, it would seem that this objection is perhaps too facile. For, at the point at which this discussion is introduced, it seems that Berkeley is merely repeating the accepted doctrine concerning the absolute invisibility of distance in the actual line of sight. That is, Berkeley seems here to be led into a rash assertion in order to gain the confidence of the optic writers in order to use what is already accepted as the starting point for his own critical investigations of the theory of vision. It would seem that Berkeley is trying merely to elicit the support of commonly accepted views in order to provide an explanation for the doctrine which he puts forward as one of his fundamental principles — that distance is not immediately perceived — even though his explanation of this notion differs considerably from the "orthodox" explanation.

C. Ideas of Sight and Touch

The heterogeneity of visual and tactile sense-ideas is perhaps the most profound and interesting aspect of Berkeley's new theory of vision. Berkeley begins his investigation of this phenomenon with a discussion of the hypothetical blind man who has been blind from birth, but who later acquires the power of vision. Berkeley contends that such a man would be unable to relate the visual sense-data which he has suddenly acquired with the tactile sense-data with which he has been familiar. That is, such a person would not think that the visual and the tactile sense-data have anything in common. A blind man who gained the visual capacity would not, according to Berkeley, have any idea of distance by sight. Visual phenomena would seem to him to be "in his mind". The judgment of distances or sizes by vision is acquired only by repeated experience, the kind of experience which is, of course, precluded by blindness. Hence, Berkeley argues, the man who had been born blind and had later gained his sight would be UNABLE to judge distance by vision. (Much of the speculation by Berkeley and others on the question of the perceptual experiences of those who have recovered their sight would appear to be superseded by the empirical data (treated, for example, in M. von Senden's *Space and Sight*) gathered about such experiences, data which seem to support some of Berkeley's claims.)

Berkeley's assertion that the objects of sight and the objects of touch are two distinct things or appearances is supported by two additional arguments. The only immediate objects of sight are, Berkeley claims, light and colors. But we cannot conceive of colors without visible extension or visible extension without colors. But this visual extension does not have the appearance of depth and, hence, is a two-dimensional order. Visual appearance is an arrangement of apparent figure, apparent position, and apparent magnitude. For, by sight alone, we perceive only a two-dimensional manifold. Though vision may be said to "suggest" distance or magnitude, neither distance nor magnitude are immediately perceived by sight. The primary and immediate objects apprehended by sight, according to Berkeley, do not appear to be "without the mind" or at a distance.[11] Light may be spoken of, or considered as, the condition for the possibility of vision and the visual field may be thought of as composed of a two-dimensional surface of various colors in juxtaposition. Although it has been argued[12] that the relations the qualities of light and color have are also visible, this is a view which Berkeley did not seem to adopt. Berkeley insists that relations are not and cannot be perceived. Since relations are imperceptible, they are not "ideas". For Berkeley, visual perception simply apprehends a panorama of colors and light; though the various colors perceived may be said to be in relation to one another, this relationship itself is not something which is actually perceived.

The second additional argument which Berkeley offers in order to support his view that the visual and tactile sense-ideas are heterogeneous is based on the premise that quantities of the same kind can be joined together, but that quantities of different kinds cannot be added together. That is, we can join together a green and red line, but we cannot add a visible to a tangible line. Berkeley seems to be stating that the qualities apprehended by one modality of sense are incompatible with the qualities apprehended by another modality of sense. Now, it would seem that both ordinary language and common experience support Berkeley in this contention. Thus, for example, we do not ordinarily say (or believe) that we see hardness or that we feel redness. Synaesthetic phenomena — processes in which one type of stimulus produces a secondary, subjective sensation — fall within the provinces of pathology or poetry rather than within the domain of philosophy.

Nevertheless, Berkeley claims that, for example, visible squares bear the same relationship to tangible squares as the word "square" bears to actual squares. That is, the visible appearance is a symbol for the (possible) tangible percept. Because of the habitual connection which we observe between visible squares and tangible squares, the visual appearance of a square becomes a sign or symbol for the square which could be (or would be) perceived through the sensation of touch. Just as road signs symbolize the concrete state of affairs which will be experienced ahead (say, an intersection), so, too, do the visible signs suggest or signify the tangible "state of affairs" which may be experienced. Though there is no necessary connection between the visual appearance and the tangible phenomenon, a connection is made on the basis of the experienced conjunction between the two phenomena. Visual perception apprehends one set of distinct phenomena, and tactile perception apprehends another distinct set of phenomena. Though visual and tangible "objects" cannot be, according to Berkeley's account of the matter, spatially related, there is, nevertheless, a distinct correlation between the realms of visual and tactile appearances. The temporal conjunction of visible and tangible objects is ultimately determined by experience through the process of the association of ideas. By repeated experience an associative bond is established between the two-dimensional manifold apprehended by vision and the three-dimensional realm apprehended by touch. There is, Berkeley avers, a numerical difference between the immediate objects of sight and the immediate objects of touch. Thus, though we may ordinarily speak of the identity of the visual object and the tactile object, Berkeley contends that such a manner of speaking is false. What we immediately perceive by sight is a sign for what may be experienced through the sense of touch. Berkeley seems to be saying that in the perception of a certain kind of visual form we tend to anticipate the kind of tactile phenomena we might perceive. That such an anticipation actually takes place in the process of perception can be illustrated in the following manner. A person may see what appears to be a slab of granite. He, then, consciously (or subconsciously) anticipates the touch sensations he would perceive if he approached the apparent object and actually reached out towards it. That is, it is conceivable that such a perceiver would anticipate the sensations of hardness, smoothness or coolness. If what was thought to be a slab of granite turned out to be simply a *papier mâché* construction (perhaps a piece of stage scenery), the surprise which we may assume the individual would experience after touching the object would itself seem to indicate that some kind of anticipation of tactile perceptions had taken place. Berkeley expresses the relationship between tactile and visual perception in the following way:

> Having of a long time experienced certain ideas perceivable by touch – as distance, tangible figure, and solidity – to have been connected with certain ideas of sight, I do, upon perceiving these ideas of sight, forthwith conclude what tangible ideas are, by the . . . ordinary course of nature, like to follow.[13]

Berkeley does not seem to believe that there is a similar anticipation of visual sense-data on the basis of the immediate perception of tangible sense-data. And Berkeley's neglect of such anticipations would seem to be quite reasonable since – if we are speaking about a perceiver with a capacity for apprehending visual and tactile phenomena – such an anticipation of visual sensations would rarely occur. It may, however, be admitted that the tangible perception of the figure of objects (e.g., the tangible perception of squares, circles or rectangles) would, indeed, lead us to anticipate the visual appearance of such tangible forms. But there is a great deal more inaccuracy in the anticipation of visual perceptions (say, for example, if an individual is blindfolded and is asked to identify the colors or color of the object he is touching) than there would be in the anticipation of tactile perceptions on the basis of visual perception.

It is interesting to note that Berkeley has incorporated the implicit assumption of an "ordinary course of nature" into his discussion of perception. Berkeley assumes that our present experiences are like our past experiences and that our future experiences will resemble our past experiences. That is, he has assumed the uniformity of nature. But, as we shall see, he does not adopt a regularity theory of causation.

For the finite perceiver the anticipation of experience is based upon the belief in the validity of the habitual associations of the past. Ultimately, the "connections" which we make between visual phenomena and tactile phenomena are purely arbitrary. That the connection we make between visual sense-data and tactile sense-data is veridical is something which we cannot know with apodictic certainty. The only guarantee that such is the case is the existence of, and goodness of, God or a supramundane consciousness.

Although the "connection" between "ideas" which has often been observed seems to indicate a causal relationship, there is no observed necessary connection between the ideas of sight and the ideas of touch. Anticipating Hume, Berkeley seems to be saying that the interpretation of a merely arbitrary connection as a necessary connection is simply the result of a determination of, or habit of, the mind which arises out of perceptual experiences of the past. The relationship which we "discover" between data of one sense and those of another is established by analogy and by experience.[14] There is, then, no "idea" which is common to visual sense-data and tactile sense-data. Thus, the visual shape of an object is distinctly different from the tangible shape of an object. If, for example, we refer to a tangible and a visible shape as "square" we are not, according to Berkeley, referring to the SAME thing. Berkeley once again considers the case of a man who had been born blind but who subsequently gained the capacity to see.[15] Such a person, it is assumed, would be accustomed to describe an object as "square" on the basis of certain tactile sensations. The question which Berkeley raises is whether the man who had previously been blind would identify a square object as such if he did not rely on tactile sensations. Berkeley contends that he would not be able to do so. Such an individual, it is asserted, would be unable to relate this visual appearance (of a square) with his tactile perceptions of square objects. To be sure, Berkeley would probably maintain that this individual (who has suddenly acquired the power of vision) would, in time, be able to "connect" the visual sense-data and the tactile sense-data on the basis of repeated experiences of the association between these modalities of sense. In regard to this point, G. J. Warnock claims that the inability of the blind man immediately to identify the visual appearance as a square arises simply from the fact that he had been blind. Through past experiences he has learned to describe objects as square on the basis of tactual perception alone. He has not learned, as those who always possessed sight have, to designate objects as square on the basis of what is perceived by both sight and touch. Since such an individual has previously never seen anything at all, he has, quite naturally, no idea of how our description of things refers to that which is seen.[16] It is interesting to note that a good deal of the empirical evidence gathered by M. von Senden in his *Space and Sight* tends to support Berkeley's contention.[17]

In regard to Berkeley's notion that there are no tactile sense-data or visual sense-data which have a specific resemblance to one another, it has been asserted[18] that the ideas of succession and co-existence are exceptions to this. It is claimed that we may describe a succession of occurrences in the field of vision and that we can also describe a succession of "felt happenings". Since we are able to speak of "succession" in both cases, it would appear that visual succession is not specifically different from tactual succession. To be sure, we may be said to experience a succession of, or concatenation of, visual phenomena as well as a succession of tactile phenomena. In all probability, Berkeley would not object to such a view; that is, that we may experience a succession of tactile sensations or of visual phenomena. But he would undoubtedly object to the belief that there are "ideas of succession". For, succession is something which is not perceived at all and, hence, is not an IDEA (i.e., a sensation or sensible quality or that which is immediately perceived). Co-existence and succession, like relations, are not phenomena apprehended in perception. They could be considered to be only notions, not ideas. That is, succession and co-existence may be described as notions in accordance with the position Berkeley adopts in the *Principles*; insofar as we know or understand the meaning of these terms they are notions, or are what he calls *entia rationis*.

Before concluding our discussion of Berkeley's notion of the bifurcation between the realm of visual perception and the realm of tactual sensation, it will be appropriate to examine a few other difficulties which such a view seems to encounter.

D. The Concept of Suggestion

As we have seen, Berkeley tends to insist upon the need to distinguish between the two-dimensional manifold apprehended in visual perception and the three-dimensional field of tactual sensation. Now, at one point in his explication of the new theory of vision, Berkeley notes that some people may be led to believe that "trine dimension" is equally the object of touch and sight.[19] He admits that we have a kind of natural propensity to think that the "ideas" of distance (or "outness") and space are immediate objects of sight. But this notion, he avers, is merely a delusion which arises from the "quick and sudden suggestion of fancy" which associates the idea of distance with the visual sense-data. Such a delusion — that the idea of distance is a proper and immediate object of sight — is corrected only by REASON.

Such an assertion would seem to undermine Berkeley's *soi-disant* doctrine of suggestion, a doctrine which has been described by A. C. Fraser as " . . . the *constructive* principle of the New Theory . . . " of vision.[20] The concept of suggestion is, in general, an application of the law of association. Now, it will be remembered that Berkeley described – in the opening pages of his *Essay* – that phenomenon by which the tactile sensations experienced on the occasion of perceiving an object close to our eyes SUGGEST to us the situation of the apparent object. It would seem that, in this context of Berkeley's argument, the suggestions by which we judge the situation of objects are thought to be reliable and adequate guides for such judgment. But in the section referred to above, Berkeley maintains that the "suggestion of fancy" produces a "mere delusion", i.e., the "delusion" that distance is an immediate object of sight.

On the one hand, Berkeley seems to be saying that suggestion is a valid guide for the judgment of distance or, at least, the spatial location of apparent objects, and, on the other hand, he designates a similar suggestion elsewhere as a "mere delusion". This apparent contradiction merely highlights the ambiguity of Berkeley's conception of the perceptual process in general. He often seems to believe that there is what may be called a proto-inferential process in perception itself from which we derive our judgments. On the other hand, he often clearly asserts that there is no inference or judgment in immediate perception. In addition, he tends to describe inference as a purely cognitive function, an act of understanding or reason.

There is no doubt that there is a certain ambiguity about the description of the nature of perception in the *Essay towards a New Theory of Vision*. It is interesting to note, incidentally, that Berkeley, in his defense of his original work, *The Theory of Vision Vindicated and Explained*, seems to be aware of the ambiguity of the terms he used in his earlier work. Thus, for example, he distinguishes, at one point, between perception and judgment, suggestion and inference.[21] He proceeds to explain that things are suggested and perceived by sense alone. Inferences and judgments are acts of the understanding. Berkeley makes reference to a familiar illustration. What we immediately perceive by sight, he avers, is its primary "object", that is, light and colors. By the mediation of such immediately perceived phenomena tangible sense-ideas are perceived OR suggested. Now, this equation of perception and suggestion introduces another difficulty. That is, is suggestion an activity identical with, or implicit in, perception, or is it, as Berkeley has previously affirmed, an activity of the imagination? It would appear that Berkeley seems to have two or more concepts of suggestion. Thus, in his *Theory of Vision Vindicated and Explained*,[22] he asserts that

> . . . the mind is . . . apt to be deluded by the sudden suggestion of Fancy, which it confounds with the Perceptions of Sense . . .

Berkeley seems to describe suggestion as a function of the imagination and also as a kind of perceptual function. It would seem that suggestions of imagination seem to lead only to error or delusion while the suggestions derived from perception are apparently thought of as valid guides for judgments derived from perception. Berkeley also refers to suggestion as signification.[23] He explains that "ideas" which are often observed to be connected with other ideas are, then, considered as signs. By means of these signs, things which are not actually perceived by sense are signified or suggested to the imagination. In this sense, suggestion may be considered as an important aspect of the process Berkeley describes as mediate perception.

At any rate, Berkeley claims that if idea A has been frequently connected with idea B, idea A becomes a sign by means of which idea B is "suggested" to imagination. Berkeley seems – contrary to the distinction he makes elsewhere – to be attributing the capacity of inference to imagination rather than to understanding. It may be said that Berkeley argues that, for example, the constant conjunction between smoke and fire apprehended in perception tends to lead us to consider smoke as a sign for what may be unperceived on some occasions (e.g., fire). The question is whether the sign "suggests" to the imagination what is not actually perceived or whether we do not infer the presence of fire on the basis of what is immediately perceived (e.g., smoke).

That there is a real confusion in Berkeley's thought concerning the precise nature of suggestion can be demonstrated by referring to an illustration (which has been cited above) taken from the *Essay towards a New Theory of Vision.*[24] Berkeley claims that, after hearing a certain sound, an "idea" is immediately suggested to the UNDERSTANDING which custom or habitual experience has connected with it. It is obvious that Berkeley seems to equate what is suggested to the imagination with what is suggested to the understanding. The ambiguous and paradoxical nature of the term "suggestion" is illustrated by the way in which it is related variously to perception, imagination, or understanding. Berkeley's notion of suggestion, as presented in the *Essay towards a New Theory of Vision* and *The Theory of Vision Vindicated and Explained*, is one of the most confusing and ambiguous conceptions in his theory of perception and is yet thought to be the central notion in that theory. A conception which appears to be closely related to the "doctrine of suggestion" (and therefore relevant to an understanding of his analysis of perception) is Berkeley's concept of "praenotions".

E. Praenotions

There is one conception which seems to have a rather peculiar status in Berkeley's theory of vision. That is, the conception of "praenotions". In his discussion of the perception of distance Berkeley remarks that the various circumstances of color, shape, and kind (of appearances) guide and influence our judgments of distance. The transition from the various appearances of an object to the judgment of distance would not be effected, Berkeley implies, without praenotions which are derived from experience.[25] Again, the apparent magnitude, apparent situation and the faintness of perceived objects and our praenotions about the size, shape, kind, and nature of things combine to suggest to us tangible magnitudes.[26] Berkeley seems to mean by praenotions the preconceptions which we have acquired on the basis of past experiences. On the basis of past perceptions we tend to develop some preconceptions about the nature of common objects which serve as guides for judgments concerning present or future perceptions. Though praenotions seem to be related to experiences of the uniformity of nature, they seem to refer specifically to the uniform characteristics (or appearances) by which apparent objects are distinguished from one another. Thus, because of our previous experience of the perception of mountains we have the praenotion that, despite the apparent small size of what appears to be a mountain (perceived at a considerable distance), the object perceived is much larger than it appears to be. On the basis of such praenotions we are able to anticipate the tangible "magnitude" of various objects.

Now, the question arises concerning the accuracy of these praenotions as guides for our judgments. Thus, for example, on the basis of our praenotions concerning such a common object as, say, an apple, we may anticipate the taste the apple will have. But, of course, if what we thought was an apple was actually a wax fruit, our expectations would be unfulfilled and our praenotions would have deceived us. It would appear that the praenotions which Berkeley introduces into his theory of vision are effete guides for the interpretation of our (possible) perceptions. Berkeley seems to negate the value of praenotions in his following statement:

> . . . language being accommodated to the praenotions of men and use of life, it is difficult to express therein the precise truth of things, which is . . . contrary to our praenotions.[27]

Whatever the function or value praenotions may have for Berkeley's thought, it is interesting to note that Berkeley seems to imply, in the above statement, that there is a "precise truth of things" which is contrary to our preconceptions and, presumably, our experiences (since our praenotions are derived from our previous experiences). For, if the praenotions which we form on the basis of experience are either inaccurate or false, then it would seem that the arbitrary connections we discover between visual sense-data and tactile sense-data in experience may be at least as false or inaccurate as our praenotions.

Nevertheless, despite the uncertainty of the foundation of praenotions, they do seem to serve as rough guides for the anticipation of sensations. The concept of praenotions could conceivably be used to resolve a difficulty which D. M. Armstrong raises against Berkeley's doctrine of the distinction between visual and tactile sense-data. Armstrong claims that if we look at a stone wall which is beyond our reach, we seem to be "seeing" its roughness or hardness in a more or less direct manner. That is, the tactual properties "of the wall" seem intimately related to the sight of the wall. Now, Armstrong uses this "synaesthetic phenomenon" as an illustration of the way in which we may " . . . think solidity into the visual world", and of the way in which we may " . . . think the tangible notion of distance into the visual world".[28] Although Armstrong does not explicitly state what he means by a synaesthetic phenomenon, it is apparent that he is referring to the way in which certain sense-impressions seem to evoke anticipatory sensations. If, for example, the visual perception of, say, a lemon seems to elicit the subjective anticipations of the sensation of bitterness. At any rate, it would seem that Armstrong, in this particular illustration, is merely pointing out the way in which our preconceptions determine our anticipations of experience. If we did not have the preconception that visual appearances we designate as "stone walls" usually have certain tactile properties (hardness, roughness, etc.) we would not anticipate our tactual experiences in such a manner. Armstrong's illustration and objection, rather than refuting Berkeley's conception of the relation between visual and tactile perception, merely confirms it. Thus, even though our preconceptions may not aid us in ascertaining the "true nature of things", they, nevertheless, are practical guides for the anticipations of experience, and have a kind of functional utility.

It appears that there is an intimate relationship between imagination, suggestion, and "praenotions". It will be argued – especially in the discussion of mediate perception – that imagination has, for Berkeley, primarily a representative function. Imagination has the function of representing those "ideas" which were "originally perceived". In addition, as we shall see, imagination seems to have the function of representing possible percepts in the process of mediate perception. That is, the sense-data immediately perceived may be said to "stand for" or represent those sensory data which may possibly be perceived.

Now, if suggestion implies the way in which "ideas" immediately perceived lead us, by a process of association, to expect or anticipate possible perceptions, it is undoubtedly a process dependent upon imagination and memory. Associations between certain sensory data (immediately perceived) and other sensory data (mediately perceived) are learned through past experiences. Hence, our present mediate perception of sense-data requires a recollection of these past associations. But memory alone is not the only aspect of suggestion since possible perceptions must be, as it were, represented in imagination. For example, if I am perceiving that "collection of ideas" I have learned to identify as a wall and I anticipate how this "wall" would feel if I walked up to it and touched it, then I am imagining what my tactile sensations would be like. The association that is made between the visual sense-data and the (possible) tactile sense-data is dependent upon a memory of similar sense-experiences. Imagination and memory are the essential ingredients of the process of suggestion. The function of "understanding" in suggestion is left rather ambiguous in Berkeley's discussion of the process. All in all, the concept of suggestion emerges in Berkeley's writings as a rather complex process involving (a) the habitual experience of the association between sense-data immediately perceived and sense-data mediately perceived; (b) a recollection of these habitual experiences in the past; (c) an imaginative re-presentation of possible perceptions and perhaps (d) the unifying cognitive function of understanding which "joins together" the various aspects of the entire process of suggestion. This last assertion is, of course, a matter of speculation. For, Berkeley simply does not make it clear, as we have said, what the function of the "understanding" is in the process of suggestion. At any rate, it is believed that the imagination cannot be reduced to suggestion simply because the process of suggestion seems to be a complex process involving the interaction of memory, imagination, and reflective comprehension.

In regard to the relationship between praenotions and suggestion it may be possible to absorb the function of praenotions into the process of suggestion. Praenotions or preconceptions are derived from past sense-experience and are remembered on the occasion of present perceptual experiences. Such preconceptions seem to be little more than the "associative bonds" which have been learned from repeated experience of relationships between various sense-data. These preconceptions provide, as it were, the material by which the imagination re-presents possible perceptions. Generally speaking, it appears that the preconceptions Berkeley discusses could be described as those concepts derived from past experience which are retained in memory and which determine the percipient individual to anticipate certain sense-experiences. "Praenotions", then, do seem to reduce to the mnemonic aspect of suggestion. But, since memory is only a contributing function to the entire process of suggestion, it appears that praenotions cannot be reduced to suggestion without an oversimplification of that process.

Because of its significance for an understanding of Berkeley's analysis of perception, we will next turn our attention to another important aspect of his description of perception, his conception of *minima sensibilia*.

F. Minima Sensibilia

In his discussion of visible and tangible extension Berkeley asserts that there is no necessary connection between the two phenomena. Although we tend to believe that we apprehend the visible and tangible qualities of the same thing, Berkeley contends that we actually apprehend qualities of two distinct objects which, because these qualities are closely connected, we speak of as a single entity. The extensions perceived by sight are quite different from, and

"... have an existence very distinct and separate from", extensions perceived by touch.[29]

Berkeley believes that sensible extension is not infinitely divisible. Thus, he argues that there is a *minimum tangibile* and a *minimum visibile*. He puts forward this notion in order to preserve his assumption that there is nothing hidden in our sense-perceptions. There is, Berkeley tends to argue, no inaccessible "thing-in-itself" which, as it were, lies "behind" our sensations. The fundamental elements of perceptual apprehension are "ideas", the atomic elements from which all knowledge which is derived from experience is "constructed". Now, for Berkeley, an unperceived "idea" is a *contradictio in adjecto*. In a sense-impression there can be nothing but that which is actually discerned in it. Since our perceptual capacities are not infinite, the tangible sense-datum of extension and the visible sense-datum of extension cannot be infinitely divisible.

This notion that there is a *minimum tangibile* and a *minimum visibile* seems to involve Berkeley in a serious difficulty. Thus, for example, we may assert that either the minima which Berkeley speaks of have an extension or they do not. If these minima do have extension, it is, of course, quite possible to argue that they must have parts and are, therefore, not minima at all. For example, if we examine the *minimum visibile* of a straight line, we find that the minima are juxtaposed in the following way: MV_1, MV_2, MV_3, MV_4, etc. But the boundary between MV_1 and MV_2 is separated from the boundary of MV_2 and MV_3. That is, the second minimum (MV_2) has boundaries which can be distinguished. This implies, therefore, that it does, in fact, have parts. If, on the other hand, the minima are said to have no extension, it would then follow that no quantity of these minima could ever form an extension. If, therefore, there is a sense-impression which is not discerned in it, then such a perception cannot be composed of minima.

Now it would seem that most lines and surfaces have an appearance of continuity. On the basis of Berkeley's analysis of perception, what is immediately perceived is actually continuous and not composed of minima, visible or tangible. The *minimum visibile* and the *minimum tangibile* would seem to be merely hypothetical entities. For, if things are what they appear to be, then things are continuous (hence, not composed of juxtaposed minima). But Berkeley would seem to argue that the tangible and visible minima are actually perceived. It is assumed that, generally speaking, surfaces both "look" and "feel" continuous. If this is the case, are we to conclude that this appearance of continuity is merely illusory? Berkeley, it would seem, would have to answer "No", since he has been concerned throughout his discussion with apparent magnitude, apparent situation, etc.

Again, we may ask ourselves what a *minimum visibile* or a *minimum tangibile* would be like. Though it is mentioned by D. M. Armstrong that a pin-prick may be considered to be an illustration of a *minimum tangibile*,[30] it would appear that the sharp pain which a pin-prick would cause is not an instance of a tactual sensation which is BARELY perceived. Although a pin-prick may be considered as a minimum area of pain, the intensity of the sensation (relatively speaking) would disqualify this sensation as an illustration of a tactile experience which is almost, but not quite, imperceptible. The perception of heat might be a clearer illustration of a *minimum tangibile*. This type of illustration, however, points out the kind of difficulty which Berkeley's view encounters. For, we may assume that the perception of heat would probably vary from perceiver to perceiver and the minimal perception of heat, the *minimum tangibile*, would be difficult to discover. A massive amount of empirical data on such questions as minimum discriminable sensations has been gathered by experimental psychologists[31] since the work of G. T. Fechner in 1860. Such phenomena (*minima sensibilia*) must ultimately remain hypothetical entities for Berkeley. And, as has been shown above, such postulates present Berkeley's analysis of perception with some serious difficulties.[32] It is interesting to note that Berkeley was led to a criticism of the concept of infinitesimals in mathematics for the same reasons that he attacks the notion of the infinite divisibility of sensible extensions. He argues that *minima sensibilia* cannot be divisible because, if this were the case, we should be able to apprehend something which sensation alone could not provide. For, if infinitesimals were admitted to exist, Berkeley's notion of *minima sensibilia* would be undermined. If quantities which are neither sensible nor imaginable could be proven to exist, then Berkeley would ultimately have to revise his entire theory of knowledge.[33]

Despite the difficulties which Berkeley's notion of *minima sensibilia* seems to produce, it appears that Berkeley is intent upon conceiving of perception as the apprehension of a multiplicity of appearances. There is, however, a residual element of representationalism present in his account of the tactile objects of perception.

G. Tactile Objects of Perception

Berkeley's *Essay towards a New Theory of Vision* is fundamentally an analysis of the nature of "reality" as it is revealed in sensation, primarily in the sensations of touch and sight. He puts forward a theory of the general nature of tactual and visual appearances and their interrelationships in his analysis of the theory of vision. There appears to be one incongruous aspect of Berkeley's seminal work. That is, the problem of Berkeley's treatment of the tactile objects of perception.

In his *Essay towards a New Theory of Vision* Berkeley tends to speak of the objects of touch in a realistic manner. They are spoken of as real things which are situated in "circumambient space", which seem to BE independently of their being perceived. The objects of touch exist "without the mind", and are not dependent, for their existence, upon their being perceived. At one stage in his argument Berkeley asserts that the magnitude of an object " . . . continues always invariably the same . . . "[34] despite the fact that the visible object changes (in its appearance) as one approaches or withdraws from the tangible object. It is argued that magnitude refers essentially to "tangible magnitude".

It has often been said, with good reason, that such a position contradicts Berkeley's view expressed in the *Principles* that all our "ideas" — the *soi-disant* primary and secondary qualities — are "in the mind". Nevertheless, we must ask ourselves why, in the context of the *Essay toward a New Theory of Vision*, Berkeley argues that tangible objects exist "without the mind". It seems that Berkeley tended to describe tangible objects as "without the mind" simply because he did not want to explicate his doctrine of immaterialism in the *Essay toward a New Theory of Vision* and because he did not want to attack too many common-sense notions at once. At any rate, Berkeley, in his *Principles*, makes a passing reference to his dialectical purpose in admitting, albeit tentatively, the externality of tangible objects.[35]

The relativity of the visual perception of magnitude made it plain to Berkeley that we cannot depend upon vision for an apprehension of magnitude. When we refer to magnitude, Berkeley argues, we must refer to tangible magnitude. Thus, if we wish to discover the distance of an object which is, say, three hundred yards away, that distance can be measured by the motion of a person's body which, Berkeley avers, is "perceivable by touch".[36] Here Berkeley is, of course, including kinaesthetic sensations within the domain of sensations of touch. The kinaesthetic sensations function as cues by which we judge distance. Now, while distance is suggested by various cues, true magnitude would seem to be directly perceived (i.e., by touch). The contradictory apparent magnitudes apprehended by vision are, as it were, corrected by tactual sensations since Berkeley has tentatively treated tangible magnitude as veridical and not merely apparent.

H. The Conception of Space

It is interesting to note that, for Berkeley, space is inconceivable without the perception of tactual or kinaesthetic sensations. Visible things, it is said, are "in the mind" and " . . . take up no part of . . . external space."[37] It is rather peculiar that Berkeley actually says so little in his *Essay* about "external" or "circumambient" space, especially since it is presupposed in many of his arguments.

At one point in his discussion Berkeley asserts that the ideas of outness, distance and space are not objects of sight.[38] Since Berkeley has defined an "idea" as an immediate object of sense, we may assume that space, since it is described as an idea, is an immediate object of sense. But, as has been mentioned above, Berkeley tends to insist that space is not an object of sight. Is it, then, an object of touch? Obviously not, since space is, by its very nature, intangible. But if space is neither an object of vision nor an object of touch, how can it be an IDEA, i.e., that which is immediately perceived? Hermann Weyl claims that Berkeley has a conception of pre-spatial localization fields which are distinct for the senses of touch and vision.[39] This interpretation of Berkeley's theory of space may resolve certain difficulties concerning his actual conception of space. But the explanation seems to go far beyond anything which Berkeley has explicitly said. And he certainly does not refer directly to anything resembling "pre-spatial localization fields". In fact, in the first part of his *Essay toward a New Theory of Vision* he affirms that objects such as houses, fields and rivers " . . . take up a considerable space . . . "[40] Hence, it would seem that space is presupposed, but the origin of our apprehension of space ultimately remains unexplained.[41] That Berkeley was aware of the difficulty of his treatment of space is expressed in the following interesting comment he makes in the *Siris*:

> . . . although the moderns teach that Space is real and infinitely extended, yet, if we consider that it is no intellectual notion nor yet perceived by any of our senses, we shall perhaps be inclined to think with Plato in his *Timaeus*, that this . . . is the result of . . . spurious reasoning, and a kind of waking dream.[42]

Apparently the problem of space perplexed Berkeley so much that he was more or less forced to make what may be called an intellectual retreat. A. C. Fraser is surely too optimistic in his assertion that Berkeley has anticipated Kant in his treatment of space.[43] There is no evidence at all that Berkeley conceives of space as a pure form of intuition, an *a priori* necessary condition of sense-experience. Strictly speaking, it may be said that Berkeley has no positive, precise theory of space at all, even though it is presupposed as the "context" in which various sense-qualities appear. In his *De Motu* Berkeley avers that absolute space is simply " . . . pure privation or negation, that is, mere nothing".[44]

I. Concluding Remarks — Some Implications Of Berkeley's Theory of Vision

Berkeley has followed through with his original intentions in his *Essay toward a New Theory of Vision.* He has given an explanation of the way in which we perceive through vision the distance, magnitude, and location (situation) of objects. He has explicated the distinctions between visual sense-data and tactile sense-data, and he has argued that there is no common "idea" related to visual and tactile phenomena. Although Berkeley retains the "proper sensibles" of Aristotle (and, of course, St. Thomas Aquinas), he simply eliminates — with a flourish of Ockham's razor — the notion of a common sense (*sensus communis*) which was thought to have the synthetic function of unifying, organizing, and integrating the perceptual data derived from the "operations" of the particular senses. Contradicting the common sense notion that distance is immediately perceived, Berkeley insists that we judge distance by means of visual and tactile cues which, on the basis of past experiences, function as signs. Visual perception enables us to apprehend appearances only. The tactile sensations we experience bring us in contact with that which is "without the mind". The relationship which we tend to believe exists between visual and tactile sense-data is one which is, for us, purely arbitrary. The "course of nature", or the permanence of the physical order is, as Berkeley puts it in his *Alciphron*,[45]

> equivalent to a constant creation of particulars by a benevolent God who in this way displays His power and providence.

Without the assumption of the existence of a benevolent God, we would be left — at the conclusion of the *Essay towards a New Theory of Vision* — in a position of skepticism in regard to perceptual apprehension. If it is assumed that the course of nature could be identified as habit, this would mean, for Berkeley, that God is not necessary as transphenomenal cause of the orderly phenomena perceived by man. And this is a view which Berkeley would obviously seek to avoid. Since the relationship between the various sense-ideas apprehended by the modalities of sense is purely arbitrary for a finite percipient, without God as guarantor of the veridical character of sense-perception we would surely be left in a position of uncertainty with regard to perception itself.

The process of perception enables us to be aware of appearances only. Apparent size, apparent magnitude, apparent figure, apparent situation, etc., are all that we perceive. What we take to be immediately perceived is not what IS, but only what SEEMS to be there for us. When we speak of "ideas" or sense-impressions we are speaking about what appears to be immediately perceived. To be sure, Berkeley maintains – at least in his *Essay towards a New Theory of Vision* – that through the sense of touch we apprehend REAL figure, magnitude or situation. But the "true" nature of that which is apprehended in touch is, strictly speaking, inferred from the appearances discovered in experience. In the case of visual and tactile perception, these sense-data are what we immediately perceive. But in the case of visual perception the sense-data perceived do not represent or correspond to anything which is "without the mind". Tactile sense-data, however, are thought to correspond to, or represent, something which is external to the perceiver. But what is the nature of the tactile object? It cannot be said to have colors, or to emit sounds, or have distinct odors or tastes. For the tangible object can only possess properties which can be discovered by the sense of touch alone.

Berkeley holds that the visual sense-data – which he designates in mystical and poetic terms as "... the Language of the Author of Nature ..."[46] – simply suggest "to the mind" the touch sensations which may be perceived. Visual perception aids us in the anticipation of tactual perception. It is strange that this divine language does not enable us to apprehend "reality", but simply presents us with a panorama of appearances. A blind man is as truly aware of the objective nature of things as is anyone possessing the power of vision. Now, it is obvious that the tangible sense-data or sensations we may have are no more at a distance or "without the mind" than are visual sense-data. There seems to be no fundamental reason why Berkeley should have made such a sharp distinction between visual and tangible sense-data. The correlation which is supposed to exist between tactual sensations and the "real" qualities of things is one that is not itself discovered in perception. If color is said to be a sense-datum which is "in the mind", there is no apparent reason why hardness (or, for that matter, any tactual datum) should not also be thought of as "in the mind". In addition, it is difficult to imagine how we can be said to "know" that tangible objects truly are in "circumambient space" since space itself is not perceived at all. Again, if we are permitted by Berkeley to transcend our tactile sense-data by concluding that we are touching some real thing (which we designate by a specific name), there seems to be no reason why we should not make a similar inference about what we perceive by means of the other modalities of sense. The implications of Berkeley's analysis of vision lead to some obvious difficulties. Ultimately, the correlation between the various modalities of sense is not found in perception, *per se*, but is maintained only by an appeal to the benevolence of God.

The conclusions which Berkeley reached at the end of his *Essay towards a New Theory of Vision* provided the groundwork for, and led ineluctably to, his positive conception of immaterialism. Armed with the notion that the objects of sense are those phenomena which are immediately perceived (i.e., "ideas"), Berkeley is prepared to argue that *esse est percipi*. Ideas are the atomic, irreducible elements out of which we "construct" THINGS or some objects of knowledge. To be sure, Berkeley does introduce other ways of knowing. But, at this stage of the development of his argument he is concerned with that mode of knowledge which is dependent upon perceptual apprehension, upon immediate sense-experience.

The description of the nature of perception, as it is presented in the *Essay towards a New Theory of Vision*, is rather ambiguous. For, at times, Berkeley writes as if he conceived of perception as purely the passive receptivity of sensations. At other times, he describes perception as a kind of inferential activity, a spontaneous process of cognition. In visual perception, at any rate, we apprehend only the appearance of things; in tactual perception we apprehend the "true" nature of things. Inferences made on the basis of, say, aural perceptions, are described as acts of the understanding. But the interpretation of visual signs is described as taking place, in some way, in the process of perception itself. The relationship between cognition and perception in Berkeley's theory of vision is not clearly explicated at all. Berkeley tends to think of sense-ideas as the "true" objects of sense AND knowledge.[47] It may even be said, with some justification, that there is a tendency in Berkeley's writings to fuse the processes of perception, conception, and imagination.

In the *Essay towards a New Theory of Vision* Berkeley had laid the foundation for the development of immaterialism, the theory of knowledge and perception which appears in his *Principles of Human Knowledge* and in the *Three Dialogues between Hylas and Philonous*. I will next try to defend Berkeley against some recent criticisms and present an analysis of his concept of causality and the problem of identity (insofar as it is generated by his analysis of the perceptual process).

Notes

1 George Berkeley, *"Essay towards a New Theory of Vision*", in *Berkeley's Works*, ed. A. C. Fraser (Oxford, 1871), Vol. I, Section 1. (Hereafter the work cited will be referred to as *E.N.T.V.*).

2 Berkeley, *E.N.T.V.*, Section 4.

3 *Ibid.*, Section 9.

4 Berkeley, *E.N.T.V.*, Section 10.

5 George Berkeley, "The Theory of Vision Vindicated and Explained", in *Berkeley's Works*, ed. A. C. Fraser (Oxford, 1871), Vol. I, Section 66. (Hereafter cited as *T.V.V.E.*).

6 Berkeley, *E.N.T.V.*, Section 21.

7 Berkeley includes a reference to Descartes' *Dioptrices*, VI, 13, in "An Appendix" to his *Essay towards a New Theory of Vision; Vide: Berkeley's Works*, ed. A. C. Fraser (Oxford, 1871), I, p. 109.

8 E. J. Furlong, "Berkeley and the 'Knot about Inverted Images'", *Australasian Journal of Philosophy*, 41 (December, 1963), 306-316.

9 D. M. Armstrong, *Berkeley's Theory of Vision* (Australia, 1960), p. 52.

10 Berkeley, *E.N.T.V.*, Section 2.

11 Berkeley, *E.N.T.V.*, Section 50.

12 D. M. Armstrong, *op. cit.*, p. 55.

13 Berkeley, *E.N.T.V.*, Section 45.

14 Berkeley, *T.V.V.E.*, Section 27.

15 What has come to be called "Molyneux's problem" was brought to the attention of the philosophical public by Locke's quotation from a letter which Molyneux had sent to him. *Vide*: John Locke, *An Essay on the Human Understanding* (London, n. d.), I, ii, ix, 8.

16 G. J. Warnock, *Berkeley* (London, 1953), pp. 38-39.

17 M. von Senden, *Space and Sight*, trans. P. Heath (Glencoe, Illinois, 1960), p. 171: " . . . although the newly sighted can perceive the shapes of visual objects as different . . . they still have no idea . . . of the individual shape seen, nor can they at first say anything about it. Initially *the sense of touch* remains *still dominant*; they continually try to replace visual impressions by tactual ones, in order by their aid to recognize the object."

18 D. M. Armstrong, *op. cit.*, pp. 82-83.

19 Berkeley, *E.T.N.V.*, Section 126.

20 A. C. Fraser, ed., *Berkeley's Works*, I, p. 387.

21 Berkeley, *T.V.V.E.*, Section 42.

22 *Ibid.*, Section 52.

23 Berkeley, *T.V.V.E.*, Section 39.

24 Berkeley, *E.T.N.V.*, Section 17.

25 Berkeley, *T.V.V.E.*, Section 63.

26 *Ibid.*, Section 59.

27 Berkeley, *T.V.V.E.*, Section 35.

28 D. M. Armstrong, *op. cit.*, p. 68.

29 Berkeley, *E.N.T.V.*, Section 121.

30 D. M. Armstrong, *Berkeley's Theory of Vision*, p. 44.

31 Experiments have been made to determine the *Reiz Limen* or "stimulus threshold" for all of the modalities of sense. Because of the variations in sensitivity from subject to subject and the variations from one modality of sense to another, the stimulus threshold is always a statistical value. Experiments have also been made to determine the "minimum visible" in the measurement of visual acuity. Hecht and Mintz (1939) found that the thinnest wire (presented against a white field) that can be seen subtends 0.5 seconds of arc. *Vide*: R. S. Woodworth and H. Schlosberg, *Experimental Psychology* (New York, 1956).

32 This account of the problems which Berkeley's position encounters in regard to the conception of *minima tangibile* and *minima visibile* is indebted to D. M. Armstrong's excellent analysis of such difficulties in his *Berkeley's Theory of Vision* (Australia, 1960).

33 G. A. Johnston, "Berkeley's Logic of Mathematics", *The Monist*, 28, 26-30.

34 Berkeley, *E.N.T.V.*, Section 55.

35 George Berkeley, *The Principles of Human Knowledge* (New York, 1935) Section 44.

36 Berkeley, *E.N.T.V.*, Section 45.

37 *Ibid.*, Section 111.

38 Berkeley, *E.N.T.V.* Section 46.

39 Hermann Weyl, *Philosophy of Mathematics and Natural Science* (Princeton, 1949), p. 129.

40 Berkeley, *E.N.T.V.*, Section 3.

41 Generally speaking, Berkeley's view of space is purely negative. His particular *bête noir* is the Newtonian notion that space is the *sensorium Dei*. In the *Principles* he asserts that "When I excite a motion in some part of my body, if it be free or without resistance, I say there is *Space* . . . when I speak of pure or empty space, it is not to be supposed that the word *space* stands for an idea distinct from, or conceivable without, body and motion." *Principles of Human Knowledge* (New York, 1935), Section 116.

42 George Berkeley, *Siris*, in A. A. Luce and T. E. Jessop, eds., *The Works of George Berkeley, Bishop of Cloyne* (London, 1948), Vol. V, Section 318.

43 A. C. Fraser, "Berkeley's Idealism", *North British Review*, LXVIII, 475; *cf.* also: A. C. Fraser, ed., *Berkeley's Works*, I, p. 387.

44 George Berkeley, *De Motu*, in A. A. Luce and T. E. Jessop, eds., *The Works of Berkeley*, IV, Section 53.

45 George Berkeley, *Alciphron*, in A. C. Fraser, ed., *Berkeley's Works*, II, iv, Section 14.

46 Berkeley, *T.V.V.E.*, Section 38.

47 Berkeley, *T.V.V.E.*, Section 20.

II

Perception and Phenomena

> Does it not appear from Phenomena that there is a Being incorporeal, living, intelligent, omnipresent, who . . . sees things themselves intimately . . . and comprehends them wholly by their immediate presence to himself?
>
> Isaac Newton, *Optiks*, Query 28

A. Qualities and Sensations

In his *Principles of Human Knowledge* Berkeley outlines the fundamental kinds of "ideas" or immediate objects which provide the foundation for our knowledge. First, there are the sense-ideas which are apprehended by the various modalities of sense. Second, there are those ideas which we are conscious of in our thoughts, feelings, desires, and volitions. Third, there are the representations of the above "ideas" in imagination or memory. Berkeley claims that the first type of "objects of human knowledge" are, as he puts it, "imprinted on the senses". In regard to these objects of knowledge, it is to be noticed that the perceiver is passive and receptive to the impressions which "affect" or are "imprinted" upon his senses, and which have their origin and source in that which is other than the perceiver. Nevertheless, Berkeley describes all sensible things as simply "collections of ideas". We designate one collection of ideas by a specific name because we have observed these ideas in combination quite often in the past. The question raised by Berkeley's equation of a "collection of ideas" with a sensible thing will be dealt with in some detail elsewhere.

In regard to the second class of objects of knowledge, the "ideas" of which we are conscious in our thoughts, feelings, desires and volition, there has been some degree of controversy surrounding Berkeley's incorporation of "operations of the mind" under the rubric of IDEAS.[1] It has been pointed out by some commentators on Berkeley that he has apparently spoken of the objects known by attending to the passions and operations of the mind as if they were ideas – immediate objects of perception or the volitional products of imagination – even though he contends elsewhere that the operations of the mind are not "ideas", but notions. There is no doubt that if we held Berkeley to his description of the second class of objects of knowledge, there would seem to be an apparent contradiction in his position. But it may be said that Berkeley's incorporation of operations of the mind in the second class of objects of the mind is, in all probability, simply a "slip of the pen". The best evidence that can be provided that this may be the case is the statement he makes in *De Motu* in which – after asserting that the imagination is the faculty which represents sensible things – he asserts that

> Pure intellect . . . is that faculty . . . concerned with spiritual and in-extended things, such as our minds, their states, passions, virtues, and such like.[2]

Berkeley's considered position would be that we have no "idea" of the mind or its "operations" or, for that matter, other minds. Given Berkeley's definition of the conception of idea, it is inconceivable that our own mind (or the mind of any other finite being), its functions or operations, could ever be described as ideas.

At any rate, Berkeley argues that besides the various IDEAS there is something which "knows or perceives" such ideas. Now, it is interesting to note that Berkeley has, *ab initio*, indicated that the term "idea" is used in order to designate what is known AND what is perceived. It is this dual function of the concept of idea which leads to a great deal of ambiguity in Berkeley's writings.

Nevertheless, Berkeley argues that the multiplicity of sense-ideas is perceived by (or known by) an active being which he describes as "*mind, spirit, soul*, or *myself*."[3] By implication he seems to be saying that there is an "I perceive" or an "I think" which, in Kantian language, must be able to accompany all of my "ideas". Although the self or mind is not, of course, itself an object of perceptual apprehension, it is presupposed as the underlying unity which apprehends the multiplicity of sense-data. The self, at any rate, cannot be considered, at this stage of Berkeley's argument, as an object of knowledge since it is not included in the catalogue of objects of knowledge which Berkeley provides in the first paragraph of the *Principles*.

The "ideas of imagination" are, of course, completely mind-dependent. Images or thoughts presuppose something which HAS these images of thoughts. The third class of objects of knowledge are the "results" of the productive capacity of the human mind (i.e., they are "products" of the will). Ideas of imagination are thought to have a representative function and to be dependent upon sense-perception. The imagination, then, has the capacity to represent that which has been (or could be) perceived by sense.

In regard to the sense-ideas which are perceived, it must be emphasized that the mode of the *percipi* is a purely passive mode of being. The structural characteristics of the existent (apprehended in sense-perception) are relativity and passivity. The perceived existent is contingent upon, and relative to, its being perceived. The mode of being of the perceived is, then, distinct from, and other than, the mode of being of the perceiver. The relation of the perceived (sense-phenomena) to the perceiving self is not external, but internal. To attempt to think away this relation is to attempt to think away the perceptual data. (i.e., of sense-data) entirely. In every perceptual situation there is a relationship between two heterogeneous phenomena: mind and the sensible, "active" subject and passive object. The absolute existence of sense-data — unrelated to a perceiver — Berkeley argues, is unintelligible. What we immediately perceive by sense are our own sense-ideas or sensations. All the ostensible qualities of things — heat, cold, hardness, extension, figure, size, etc. – are nothing but so many " . . . sensations, notions, ideas, or impressions . . . "[4] Now, it is at once obvious that Berkeley indicated, in this equation of sensations, notions, ideas, and impressions, a certain imprecision in the use of fundamental terms. Just as he has equated perception and understanding (when, for example, he speaks of objects " . . . being perceived by the understanding)",[5] so, too, has he equated sensations with notions. Despite the apparent imprecision in terminology which Berkeley's remarks seem to indicate, he insists, nonetheless, that the existence or being of a sensible thing or object is inseparable from its being perceived.

Although Berkeley himself had retained, at the conclusion of his *Essay toward a New Theory of Vision*, a form of the representational theory of perception in so far as he admitted that tangible sense-data represent, copy or resemble things which exist external to the mind, he proceeds, in the *Principles of Human Knowledge*, to attack the notion that sense-ideas represent anything which is other than, or distinct from, sense-ideas themselves. Specifically, he argues that sense-ideas do not resemble or copy things which exist outside consciousness in an unthinking material substance. He insists that sense-data are like other sense-data alone. Thus, for example, a sound cannot be like something which is inaudible, nor can a scent be like something which is odorless. If, Berkeley says, someone argues that our sense-data are "pictures" of some external object or thing, then our sense-data will be "like" things which are completely "unlike" our sense-data themselves. If, on the other hand, an opponent claims that the objects which our sense-data copy are themselves perceivable, then these objects are sense-data. Such a position, however, simply supports Berkeley's assertions and supplies additional evidence that what we perceive are sense-data.

To perceive, according to Berkeley, is to apprehend a multiplicity of ideas which are "imprinted" on our senses. Since Berkeley insists that by "idea" he means that which has some relationship to a mind or spirit, it is impossible for an unperceiving thing, an inert substratum, to "have" ideas. Berkeley tends to argue that qualities have only a relative and dependent existence. Hence, individual or particular qualities are perceived by and are relative to a particular mind. "Ideas" cannot exist apart from some mind.

Although the multiplicity of sense-ideas apprehended in perception may be said to be "given" to a percipient being insofar as they are not simply "creatures of his will", they are, nevertheless, dependent upon a perceiver for their mode of existence. Sense-ideas do not have any "subsistence" without the mind. To refer to an inaccessible "material substratum" which is invisible and unobservable as the "support" of sensible qualities is to introduce an occult entity which, as it were, "lies behind or beneath" the ideas which are or may be perceived. Berkeley maintains that there is no need to introduce such an occult entity into an analysis of perception.

Berkeley's critique of the representational theory of perception naturally leads him to a consideration of the distinction which had been made – by Galileo and Locke – between primary and secondary qualities. It was believed that the primary qualities – rest, motion, solidity, extension, figure, etc. – were objective qualities of things or, as Berkeley puts it, " . . . patterns or images of things which exist without the mind". These primary qualities of course, were thought to inhere in a material substratum, what Locke described as the ". . . supposed, but unknown support of those qualities we find existing, which we imagine cannot subsist . . . without something to support them".[6]

The so-called secondary qualities – colors, sounds, scents, tastes, etc. – were thought of as subjective, as existing "in the mind". Berkeley's method of argument takes the form of insisting that the primary or "original" qualities cannot be separated in thought from the secondary qualities. Thus, the reader is challenged to attempt to conceive of extension without shape or without color. Since the primary and secondary qualities are inseparable, they are both "in the mind and nowhere else".

Berkeley insists that the same kind of arguments which are used in order to illustrate the mind-dependent status of secondary qualities can be applied to an analysis of the primary qualities. Thus, extension or figure are not resemblances of things which exist outside or "without" the mind because the perception of extensions or figures varies in relation to the situation of, or condition of, the perceiver. The perception of figure, for example, results in a variety of contradictory appearances which, again, are dependent upon the condition of, or the situation of, the percipient.

In his *Three Dialogues between Hylas and Philonous* Berkeley tries to argue that sensations are a fundamental class of mind-dependent sense-data, and that sensible qualities are equally as mind-dependent. Berkeley takes the case of the sensation of heat as a paradigm case of the mind-dependent status of sensible qualities. Berkeley argues that an extreme degree of heat is experienced as pain. Hence, it is a sensation which is immediately experienced. The sense-idea of heat, an ostensible sensible quality, is, then, completely mind-dependent; that is, it is dependent upon a perceiver who is receptive of this datum. Though it is obvious that Berkeley has here taken a particular case of the mind-dependent nature of an apparent sensible quality which is quite plausible, it has been argued that Berkeley's *soi-disant* "argument from sensation" would not hold its own in regard to other sensible qualities. D. M. Armstrong has presented a number of arguments against Berkeley's contention that sensible qualities are as mind-dependent as sensations. His fundamental objections may be summarized as follows:

(a) Sensible qualities are perceived, but sensations are had or are FELT. The *esse* of sensations is not *percipi*, but *sentiri*. Hence, Berkeley is mistaken in his assertion that sensations cannot exist unperceived.

(b) Though it is quite possible that the perception of sensible qualities may be a case of misperception, it is inconceivable that a similar mistake could be made in regard to an experienced sensation. Though we may not be able to identify the cause of a specific sensation, we are, nevertheless, certain that the sensation is experienced. Thus, sensations are in an entirely different category than are what we describe as sensible qualities.

(c) Sensible qualities are perceivable by any number of percipients who are "suitably placed", but sensations are private.

(d) The sensible qualities of things continue to be sensible qualities of those things even though there is no one actually perceiving them. But a sensation cannot exist unexperienced or "unfelt". Thus, it would seem, for all of these reasons, that sensible qualities cannot be considered as sensations.[7]

It would appear that a reasonable defense of Berkeley's position could be made against all of these objections. In the first place, Berkeley is not specifically interested in EQUATING or IDENTIFYING sensible qualities and sensations. Though it must be admitted that in the illustration he offers – the intimate relationship between intense heat and the sensation of pain – it would seem that this is his intention. Yet, Berkeley is simply intent upon showing that sensible qualities as well as sensations are sense-ideas or are immediately perceived. Berkeley argues in such a way as to attempt to show that sensations AND sensible qualities do not exist without any relationship to a perceiver. In effect, he attempts to argue that sensations and ostensible sensible qualities are both mind-dependent. If this is the case, then Berkeley is quite consistent when he includes both sensible qualities and sensations under the rubric "ideas". Even if we grant some substance to Armstrong's objections to Berkeley's position, it is still possible to defend Berkeley against such attacks.

In regard to Armstrong's first objection, it may be said that Berkeley includes under the rubric "perception" both the so-called sensible qualities of things and sensations. Sensible qualities are, for Berkeley, "imprinted" on our senses and, hence, are as mind-dependent as are sensations. According to him, we perceive color, figure AND pain. In accordance with Berkeley's notion of perception, to say that sensations can exist unperceived would be to assert a contradiction in terms. Perception is thought by Berkeley to be a "passion". Hence, sensible qualities and sensations are both perceived. If Armstrong wants to substitute an alternative notion of perception, he is, of course, free to do so; but his interpretation of the nature of perception is not Berkeley's. Armstrong's distinction between *sentiri* and *percipi* is one which Berkeley would have challenged.

Armstrong's second objection incorporates an assumption found in his first objection to Berkeley's position. That is, that sensations belong to an entirely different category than sensible qualities. Now, it is believed that Berkeley was aware of the phenomenological distinction between sensible qualities and sensations, but he, nevertheless, insisted that both are perceived. Since he has described perception as a passive, receptive process, he asserts that sensible qualities and sensations are both "given", are both "imprinted" on our senses. In general, it may be said that, according to Berkeley, sensations and sensible qualities are both sense-impressions. When Berkeley discusses the perception of heat and tries to show that the assimilation of a sensible quality to a sensation is plausible, it is believed that he is not primarily determined to destroy the distinction between sense-qualities and sensations (though, as we have said, this may SEEM to be his intention). Rather, he is trying to show the similarity between sense-qualities and sensations by indicating that both are given to a percipient being, both are, in the broadest sense of the term, "impressed" upon a perceiver's sensory organs and both are intimately related to a percipient being. Because of these similarities, Berkeley does not hesitate to include both sensible qualities and sensations under the rubric "ideas". Even D. M. Armstrong admits that

> Berkeley might . . . argue that the example of feeling heat shows that feeling is a species of perception. For this reason, our use of the word "perceive" in the case of sensible qualities does not, by itself, suffice to show that Berkeley is wrong in assimilating the two classes of things to each other.[8]

At any rate, Armstrong also claims, in this second objection to Berkeley's position, that the perception of sensible qualities can be an instance of misperception. Now, it appears that Berkeley does not deny this in regard to mediate perception, but he did deny that immediate perception could possibly be a case of misperception. Immediate perception is, for Berkeley, as indubitable as is immediate sensation. Thus, the immediate perception of sensible qualities and the immediate perception of sensations is, according to Berkeley, the indubitable apprehension of a sense-idea. And, of course, sense-ideas are mind-dependent by definition.

In this same objection Armstrong argues that though it is possible for there to be cases of misperception of sensible qualities, it is not possible for us to be wrong about sensations which are experienced. He claims that if an individual perceives that an object is colored grey, it makes sense for such an individual to say that the object is not grey, but only seems grey. In the case of the sensation of pain, Armstrong argues, an individual may be mistaken about the location of the pain which is experienced; he cannot be mistaken about the sensation itself.

Now, Berkeley undoubtedly would have agreed with Armstrong about the indubitability of the sensation of pain. But he would also assert that though it may "make sense" to say that something appears grey or seems grey, such assertions imply a JUDGMENT ABOUT what is perceived and, in no way, detract from the notion that sense-qualities which are immediately perceived are as indubitable as are sensations.

The third objection which Armstong puts forward against Berkeley's views on perception again assumes that Berkeley intended to equate sensible qualities with sensations. Now, in the first place, the fact that sensible qualities are capable of being perceived by many percipients and sensations are "had" uniquely by an individual does no damage to Berkeley's essential position. Sensible qualities are perceived by many finite percipients and are dependent for their existence upon their being perceived. Sensations and sensible qualities both have a mind-dependent "status". Hence, they are both species of "ideas". Berkeley would probably be receptive to the notion that sensible qualities and sensations are distinct. But even if he were willing to grant this, he would still insist that they do have one thing in common; that is, they depend upon a percipient being for their relative mode of existence.

Armstrong's fourth objection to Berkeley is not actually an objection at all since all he does is to substitute a counter-statement directed against Berkeley's position. Berkeley would argue that an unperceived sensible quality would be a contradiction in terms. The very existence of sensible qualities depends upon their being perceived by finite percipients (or their being known by the divine mind). Berkeley undoubtedly would argue that just as it is inconceivable for anyone to assert that a sensation can "exist" unexperienced so, too, is it equally inconceivable that a sensible quality could be said to BE even though it is unperceived.

At any rate, Berkeley argues, in defense of his conception of the mind-dependent nature of primary and secondary qualities, that we do not know, BY SENSE ALONE, what the true or real extension or color of objects is. Against those who aver that extension is nothing but a modification of, or accident of, a material substance, Berkeley argues that even if it were possible for figured, solid, or movable substances to exist independent of the mind – substances which "correspond" to the sense-idea we have of bodies – it would be impossible for us to know this. We cannot know it by means of sensation; but we are cognizant only of our sensations (i.e., what is immediately perceived by sense). Whether our sensations resemble or copy something which is other than that which is immediately perceived is something which, in the process of perception alone, we cannot discover. Hence, if we have any knowledge at all of "external" things, this species of knowledge must be derived from reasoning alone.

We may infer, for example, the existence of what is unperceived on the basis of what is immediately perceived. But, Berkeley argues, such an inference presupposes that there must be some external cause for our sense-ideas or sensations. We are aware, however, of experiencing "sensations" in dreams, illusions, etc., which, we believe, have no external cause and do not resemble external bodies. Hence, we need not suppose the existence of external bodies which are necessary for the "production" of our sense-ideas.

At this point in his argument Berkeley is intent upon attacking what may be described as the traditional causal theory of perception.

B. The Causal Theory of Perception

What has been described as the causal theory of perception states, fundamentally, that our sense experiences are causally dependent upon physical processes or physical objects which are not directly perceived. The subjective awareness of the "modifications" of our perceptual organs (or brain) it is thought, corresponds to, and is causally related to, a physical process or physical object which is distinct from the perceiver. An essential presupposition of the causal theory of perception is simply that the nature or character of our sensations or sense-data provides us with good reason to believe that they are dependent upon some external causes.

As is the case with Berkeley, the argument from illusion has often been pressed into service in order to demonstrate that it is false to believe that anyone ever directly perceives a material object. The passive and receptive character of the perceptual process suggests that the sensations which are experienced are caused by something extrinsic to the perceiver. Sense-data "imprinted" on our senses may be thought of as events. Now, we naturally tend to believe that all events have a cause (or causes). We assume, then, that a specific perceptual event is caused by (a) the perceiver himself, or (b) by something other than the perceiver. The commonsense notion is, in general, that a material object is the cause of our sensations or perceptions.

Berkeley argues that there is no reason to believe that the sense-data we are affected by are caused by, or dependent upon, the absolute existence of material bodies or substances. On the basis of what Berkeley describes as " . . . dreams, frenzies, and the like . . . "[9] we may be tempted to believe that our sense-data are produced sometimes and may possibly be always produced in the precise order in which we presently perceive them without assuming any concurrence between our sense-data and some external object, body, or substance which is thought to cause these data.

It is interesting to note that, at this stage of his argument, Berkeley has not introduced any distinction between dream-states and the conditions of ordinary perception. He assumes, at least for dialectical purposes, that the order and succession of sense-data in dreams or in "frenzies" is indistinguishable from the order and succession of sense-data experienced under "ordinary" perceptual conditions. It is quite possible that Berkeley's appeal to dream-states and/or frenzies in this instance could be construed as damaging not only to his opponents' views, but to his view that sense-data are caused by a divine Being. A consistent pursuit of the analogy between dream-life and waking life could conceivably be quite damaging to Berkeley's position. For, it would appear that in dreams we tend to assume that the sense-data perceived at the time are actually caused by "things" existing outside ourselves. Upon waking, we discover that the ostensible objects which we dreamt about are not present to our awareness. But if we hold Berkeley to his analogy, it would seem that we have no reason to suppose that there is any EXTERNAL cause of the sense-data we experience in a waking state (if, as Berkeley tends to suggest, the order and succession of phenomena in dream-states or frenzies is THE SAME AS the order and succession of phenomena we ordinarily perceive under "normal" conditions). It would seem that, in his polemic against those who assert that our sense-data are caused by material substances, Berkeley tends to use his argument from dreams and frenzies with some success; but he must, in the exposition of his own position, present specific criteria by which we can distinguish dream-states from "ordinary" or "normal" perceptual conditions.

Nevertheless, Berkeley does introduce a form of the causal theory of perception which may be described as spiritual causation. Before he does so, however, he dismisses the possibility that the sense-data themselves are the cause of our sensations. Because of the inactive and powerless nature of such sense-ideas as extension, figure, and motion, it is inconceivable, according to Berkeley, that they could possibly be the cause of our sensations. The being of the *percipi*, as we have seen, is passive. An examination of our sense-ideas and our "ideas of imagination" reveals that they are devoid of power, agency or activity. An "idea" (sensation or sensible quality) cannot, by definition, be the cause of anything. Hence, the perceiver is in a passive and receptive condition in relation to passive and inert sense-data which are, nevertheless, "imprinted on the senses".[10]

The perception of a continual succession of sense-data which change, which come into being and pass away, Berkeley argues, leads us to believe that there is a cause of these sense-data. This cause must be such that it produces and changes these phenomena and is independent of the phenomena which are dependent upon it. Such a cause cannot be a quality-idea or a "collection of ideas" (a thing). Hence, it must be a substance. Not, as it has been shown, a material substance, but a spiritual substance.[11] A spirit or spiritual substance is defined by Berkeley as a simple, undivided, ACTIVE being. Implicitly, Berkeley has incorporated a Leibnitzean definition of substance as: *Un être capable d'action.* Refining this notion of spirit, Berkeley asserts that in its perceptive function or capacity "spirit" is designated as the UNDERSTANDING. (Note the recurrence of the tendency to fuse the processes of perception and conceptualization which is found in the *Essay toward a New Theory of Vision*.)

We are told, then, that the understanding has the function of perceiving sense-data. But, it may be asked, are we also to believe that the understanding is passive and receptive *vis-à-vis* sense-data? Now, if the understanding is passive in the process of perception, it cannot itself be the cause of sense-data. Berkeley avoids this difficulty by discussing that aspect of consciousness – its productive capacity – which he designates as WILL.

At any rate, it would seem that we cannot have an "idea" of the spirit or self since it cannot itself be perceived. Berkeley argues, however, that we have a notion of spirit and its various operations.

We can be said to know such notions insofar as we understand the meaning of the words. But it would seem that, by the same criterion, the materialist could say that he had a notion of matter since he understands the meaning of the word. Again, it may be said that one knows the meaning of the term IDEA. Does this mean that idea is itself a notion? On the basis of the criterion by which Berkeley has described notions there seems to be no reason why the concept of idea itself – the central conception in Berkeley's thought – should not be included under the category of notion. For, the idea itself is no more discovered in perception than is, say, relation. To be sure, there are sense-data, "ideas of imagination". But the term "idea" must be, ultimately, an *a priori* category since it is "independent" of experience and it is not derived from experience. That is, the conception of idea is a general category under which a group of diverse, particular sensations and qualities are subsumed. The various phenomena apprehended in immediate perception are grouped together under the category of "ideas" and are, despite their phenomenological diversity, "unified" in the understanding by being subsumed under a category which is not itself an immediate perceptual datum.

Nevertheless, in his attempt to delineate the manner by which sense-data are "imprinted on the senses", Berkeley argues that there is undoubtedly a cause of the sensations (or sense-data) which we perceive. This cause cannot be the supposed, unthinking, inactive material substance which the materialists describe. That which is described as inert and inactive cannot be the cause of anything. The active and productive capacity of the human will illustrates a mode of "exciting" or creating "ideas" in the mind which, for Berkeley, is an analogue for the phenomenon of spiritual causation.[12] To be sure, the finite mind can only produce "ideas of imagination", the phantasms which are created at will. But we cannot will what we see, hear or smell. In relation to sense-data the finite consciousness is passive and receptive.

Since the finite percipient is passive in relation to the sense-data he perceives, Berkeley avers, he must be receptive to sense-data created by, or produced by, a "will or spirit". How, it may be asked, are we to distinguish between the sense-data which are, in Berkeley's metaphor, "imprinted" on our senses and the "ideas of imagination" which are merely the phantasms produced by our own volition? In order that such distinctions may be made, Berkeley attempts to set forth the criteria by which we are able to distinguish the "chimerical" from the real.

C. The Chimerical and the Real

Berkeley offers the following criteria by which, it is said, we are able to distinguish between sense-ideas and ideas of imagination: sense-ideas are stronger, livelier, and more distinct than are the phantasms of imagination. In addition, sense-data are identified by their steadiness, order, and coherence. Again, sense-data are not (as are "ideas of imagination") "excited at random".[13] Rather, they appear in orderly concatenation. Sense-data are external to the perceiver insofar as they are not the products of, or creations of, the perceiver's consciousness. But, it would seem that the criteria by which Berkeley would distinguish sense-data from imagined "ideas" present some difficulties for his position.

Berkeley asserts that sensory data are orderly, coherent, lively, etc. Now, it is quite possible that imagined "ideas" may have the same characteristics as sense-data. If this were not the case, the subjective impact and psychological power of images (or imagined scenes) would be inexplicable. Thus, for example, if we imagine a particularly joyous occasion in the past, the images we produce may very well be orderly, coherent, lively, etc. There is no strictly neutral evidence to which to appeal in order that we may distinguish imagined "ideas" from sense-data. It is interesting to note that Berkeley himself, at times, seems to feel that there is no significant difference between sense-ideas and imagined ideas. Thus, in a passage referred to above, Berkeley asserts that

> . . . it is granted on all hands (and what happens in dreams, frenzies, and the like, put it beyond dispute) that *it is possible we might be affected with all the ideas we have now, though there were no bodies existing without, resembling them.*[14]

The attempt to determine the distinctions between the "real" and the "chimerical" introduces some difficulties into Berkeley's theory of knowledge. For, to begin with, the real cannot truly be distinguished from the unreal by any relation between the "idea" in consciousness and the supposed independent object, but only by some relation found within experience itself. Berkeley provides, then, experiential criteria by which we can distinguish the real from the unreal. His experiential criteria are the following: first, the sense-data are independent of the will of the perceiver; second, sense-data are livelier than, more vivid than, the ideas of imagination; and third, the real is experienced as an interconnection of veridical perceptions in accordance with the "laws of nature". Now, it is interesting to note that only the last of these criteria would be sufficient in the specific cases of hallucination or simple errors of observation or illusions. In regard to the first criterion, it is difficult to imagine how we could know that the sense-data we are perceiving are independent of our will. To be sure, it is obviously the case that certain images or imagined scenes are the result of volition. We are aware of our own activity in imaginative reconstructions of the past or imaginative anticipations of the future. And, precisely because we are self-consciously aware of ourselves as the origin and cause of our phantasies, we naturally distinguish between such "day-dreaming" and the ostensible reality we ordinarily experience. But this may not be the case with all "ideas of imagination".

In hallucination, for example, we have an instance in which "ideas of imagination" are extremely vivid and absorbing. Even if an individual is aware that he is experiencing an hallucination, the perceived phenomena still have the appearance of being "given". The schizophrenic patient will become so engrossed in an hallucination that his attention cannot be directed to anything other than what he is experiencing. The terror experienced by those suffering from avitaminosis as a result of chronic alcoholism is adequate testimony to the startling intensity of the hallucinatory experience. It is obvious that an hallucination is as REAL for the individual experiencing it as the so-called public object which is inter-subjectively perceived. Again, a person who experiences an illusion is, at the time during which he is having this experience, as certain that the data he is perceiving are not simply products of his consciousness as is the person who is passively receptive to sense-data "imprinted" on his senses.

In regard to the criterion of vividness, it may simply be said that the vividness of hallucinations, dreams, etc., is characteristic enough to need no explication. The criterion of vividness, it would seem, is undoubtedly the weakest of Berkeley's criteria for distinguishing ideas of imagination from sense-data.

In regard to the criteria of coherence, order, regularly, constancy, and concatenation it would seem that there is a certain circularity involved. For, Berkeley argues that the order, coherence, steadiness, etc., of the sense-data we experience lead us to believe that there is a supra-finite being who is the cause of these phenomena. The characteristics of the sense-data mentioned above are, Berkeley claims, adequate testimony to the benevolence of the spiritual cause of these ideas, God. But, on the other hand, the existence of such a supra-finite spirit is presupposed as the author of the laws of nature which finite individuals apprehend only on the basis of past experience. But, as Berkeley admitted in his *Essay towards a New Theory of Vision*, the interconnection and correlation between the various modalities of sense is guaranteed only by the existence of a benevolent God. Therefore, Berkeley seems to argue from the orderly, coherent, steady concatenation of sense-data to the necessary existence of a supra-finite spirit who, nevertheless, must be presupposed as the benevolent cause of the observed order, coherence, and regularity of sense-data.

There is an additional and tangential question which seems to arise out of this discussion. If the "laws of nature" are learned "by experience", why is it necessary to introduce a supra-finite Being who is the support of, and creator of, these laws of nature? There would seem to be no need to introduce a divine Being as the ground and cause of the laws of nature if finite beings are capable of DISCOVERING the laws of nature on the basis of their own experiences. Nevertheless, in regard to the above discussion it must be admitted that neither the relation to the external cause (of sense-data), the ostensible independence of volition nor the "fixed order of nature" constitute adequate criteria by which a nature fundamentally different from "ideas of imagination" can be attributed to sensations or sense-data. Nevertheless, Berkeley insists, in his *Principles*, that the phenomena which are imprinted on our senses by "the Author of nature"[15], sense-data, are alone described as "real things".

Berkeley argues that our sensations – no matter how vivid or distinct they may be – exist in consciousness or are perceived by a finite being in the same way in which "ideas of imagination" are. To be sure, Berkeley insists that the sense-ideas are more real than – i.e., are stronger than, more livelier than, more coherent than – imagined ideas. Berkeley asserts that sense-data are "less dependent" upon the finite being which perceives them in so far as they are caused by, or are dependent upon, the will of a "more powerful spirit". Now, it would seem that sense-data are not merely LESS DEPENDENT upon the finite percipient than are the "ideas" of imagination. For, Berkeley has argued that when we open our eyes we perceive phenomena whether we will to or not. Hence, sense-data are completely independent of the perceiver since they are said to be caused by an infinite spirit. Perhaps Berkeley was led to say that sense-data are less dependent upon a finite spirit for their "existence" because he is aware that he has described finite beings as completely passive in the perception of sensory data. This admission – which is implicit in much of what Berkeley says about sense-perception – is, it would seem, incompatible with his notion that TO BE is not only TO BE PERCEIVED, but TO PERCEIVE. In the *Principles*, for example, Berkeley asserts that " . . . a . . . spirit is an active being, whose existence consists, not in being perceived, but in perceiving ideas and things."[16] That a finite being is active in perception is an impression which is not clearly apparent in much of what Berkeley has said about perception.

As a matter of fact, it would seem that the finite mind is active essentially in the "creation" of ideas of imagination. It is interesting to note that, for Berkeley, it is precisely in the random creations of phantasms or images, in the act of willing, that the finite being asserts its existence most clearly. Power or agency belong only to beings with the capacity of volition. Berkeley, it would seem, comes quite close to affirming a Cartesian notion: *Volo ergo sum*, "I will, therefore, I am." There is a strong Cartesian element in Berkeley's thought which is especially evident in his tendency to incorporate all mental activities – willing, imagining, sensing, and thinking – under the rubric of perception. While Descartes tends to center the existence of the finite being upon the specific mental acts of doubting or thinking, Berkeley places his emphasis upon the activity of willing. Nevertheless, it is on the basis of an analogy with our own volitional activity that Berkeley argues that there must be a "spirit" which causes our own sense-perceptions.

The veracity of sense-ideas is dependent upon the existence of a benevolent God. Indeed, the sense-data which are experienced present a "rational discourse" of the governing spirit of God. God, then, is the efficient cause of sense-data which are "imprinted" on the senses of finite beings. To some this has seemed a rather bizarre explanation of the ground of, or cause of, perceptions. It has often been argued that Berkeley has somewhat arbitrarily substituted God as cause of our sensations for the far simpler notion that material substance is the cause of what we perceive. J. Wild has asked how the most immediate sensations justify any inference to that which is completely other than a sensation and which is totally beyond our immediate experiences. Again, if we grant that there is such a being who causes our sensations, how could such a transcendent being be the "cause" of a concatenation of sense-data which are intimately linked together in a TEMPORAL succession? As Wild puts it,

It is utterly impossible to derive God causally from *my* world as to derive my world causally from God. Causation, however we choose to define it, has meaning only with respect to events in time . . .[17]

This objection bears a "family resemblance" to objections to the causal argument for the existence of God, and it does seem to have some cogency. But it would seem that Berkeley's theory of spiritual causation does save him the embarrassment of having to speak about an unknown and unknowable "something I know not what" as the efficient cause of perceptions. Of course, it does so at a metaphysical price few would be willing to pay.

Nevertheless, Berkeley does admit that the "Power or Cause" of sense-phenomena is not, strictly speaking, discovered in experience or perception at all. Rather, the spiritual cause of our sense-ideas is primarily not an object of sense, but of reason.[18] Berkeley argues that we infer the existence of, or reality of, a cause on the basis of observed effects. In general, Berkeley's view of spiritual causation is reminiscent of Malebranche's conception of causation. Malebranche insisted that all true causation is ultimately spiritual or divine. In this sense, then, Berkeley's conception of spiritual causation is apparently nothing but a modified version of that of Malebranche.[19] Berkeley has, at any rate, attempted to argue consistently that God is ultimately the efficient cause of the sense-ideas which are apprehended in sense-experience. Precisely because of this conception of spiritual causation Berkeley seems to involve himself in some difficulties concerning the relationship between the phenomenal data perceived by finite minds and the divine "ideas".

D. Phenomenal Appearances

If we grant Berkeley the metaphysical possibility of the "spiritual" causation of sense-data, it would appear that we immediately encounter a difficulty. Percepts or "ideas" are thought to exist "in the mind" of the perceiver. But, at the same time, it is also asserted that these "ideas" (or, at least, SOME of these "ideas") are caused by the divine will. Though the being of any sense-datum depends upon its being perceived, it may be asked what relation there is between the sense-datum perceived by a finite percipient and the "ideas" in the mind of an infinite spirit. Berkeley has argued that the existence of what is unperceived by finite minds is, as it were, guaranteed by the "perception" of such entities by God. Now, are we to assume that the sense-datum which may possibly be perceived by a finite percipient but is actually perceived by an infinite spirit is one and the same "idea"? If there is, as Berkeley tends to argue, a mind which affects us with all the sensible impressions we "receive", then it would seem that our own sense-impressions must be distinct from the ideas which are thought to be in the mind of such a being. It would appear that Berkeley is ultimately forced into admitting his own version of, or variation of, the representational theory of perception.

That this is the case is obvious from the admission, by Berkeley, that we cannot see things "... by perceiving that which represents them in the intelligible substance of God ... "[20] That is, Berkeley is at pains to avoid the Malebranchean notion that we "see all things in God", or have access to the contents of the divine mind. Again, he finds it incomprehensible that our own "ideas" can be the essence of, or any part of the essence of, God or the substance of God.[21] It is impossible, on the basis of what Berkeley has said, that the sense-ideas perceived by finite percipients are the same as, or identical with, the "ideas" in the mind of God. It may be concluded, then, that the sense-data presented for human perception are copies of, or resemblances of, the eternal IDEAS in the divine consciousness. Although Berkeley denies that we can actually know what is in God's mind, we must, nevertheless, insist that whatever the nature of the divine "ideas" they surely cannot be identical with the sense-data "imprinted" on the senses of finite perceivers. It is precisely because of this difficulty that Berkeley introduced the notion that what we describe as sense-ideas or things have an archetypal and eternal existence in the mind of God.

Berkeley claims that thing-ideas are preserved in God's mind. But, it may be asked, how do we know that the SAME "ideas" which are perceived by finite perceivers have an archetypal existence in the mind of God? In addition, it may be asked, how could our sense-ideas be COPIES of the divine "ideas" since the two differ in both kind and degree? In fact, it would appear that Berkeley could not claim to KNOW that our (ectypal) sense-ideas are truly copies of, or representations of the divine Ideas since the finite mind is only aware of, or conscious of, its own "contents" and never of the content of the divine mind. The archetypes are, and must be, forever hidden both from our perception and our knowledge. Now, it is obvious that many of the arguments which Berkeley has directed against the representational theory of perception could be, with equal validity, turned against his own position. The question which Philonous puts to Hylas is damaging to Berkeley's own position. "How", Philonous asks,

> . . . is it possible that things perpetually fleeting and variable as our ideas should be copies or images of anything fixed and constant?[22]

This question would seem to be especially penetrating since Berkeley has persistently argued that our sense-data are undergoing continuous change and are dependent upon the alterations in the medium, distance or "instruments" of sensation. The notion that there are archetypes which our sense-ideas copy or represent returns to haunt Berkeley's thought despite the fact that he has directed a good deal of his philosophical ammunition against precisely such a notion.

There would seem to be an even more serious objection which could be raised in regard to this aspect of Berkeley's theory of perception. Since it is assumed that the mind of God transcends time or temporal processes, that which man perceives cannot be the real things themselves, but only their appearances in a relative and temporal existence. The oft-repeated Berkeleyan doctrine that things are as they appear to be is undermined by the introduction of the archetypal "ideas". It would be quite accurate to claim that, ultimately, there are things-in-themselves in Berkeley's theory of perception. The contents of the divine mind (whether they are thought of as perceived by God or known by Him) are the true realities; the objects of sense, the sense-data perceived by a finite percipient, are only fleeting, ostensibly imperfect, copies of, or representations of, the eternal archetypes.

In the ultimate analysis of Berkeley's position it would seem that real existence is exclusively present only to God's mind. The sense-presentations, the "given", cannot be ultimately real since, by the very nature of their presentation to finite minds, they can have only a relative or transitory existence. What the finite being perceives is not what is ultimately real, but only the phenomenal manifestations of, or representations of, that reality.[23] Again, if it is admitted that what is perceived by a finite individual is not identical with what is present to the divine mind, then such "ideas" would not, ultimately, be dependent for their existence upon being perceived by finite perceivers and, hence, the essential arguments centering about the notion that *esse est percipi* – which insist upon such dependence – would be undermined. Of course, Berkeley could very well defend the notion, in accordance with his essential position, that sense-ideas have a relative existence in relation to finite perceivers, but an absolute existence in the divine mind.

It is interesting to note that A. A. Luce, though he admits that

> . . . Berkeley does not presume to define the status of that which is perceived by God and not . . . perceived by man,[24]

insists that Berkeley claims that we PERCEIVE exactly what God "perceives". Now, there would seem to be little or no evidence that such is Berkeley's "typical position".[25] In fact, such a view is incongruous with Berkeley's insistence that man cannot have access to the divine mind. Berkeley invariably attempts to deny that his view of human knowledge or perception bears any direct relationship to that of Malebranche. Especially in his *Commonplace Book* did Berkeley disagree with Malebranche's position.[26] Again, in the second of the *Dialogues between Hylas and Philonous* Berkeley asserts that " . . . there are no principles more fundamentally opposite than his [Malebranche's] and mine".[27] This opposition was most apparent in regard to Berkeley's attempt to dissociate himself from the Malebranchean notion that we "see all things" in God.

Since this is the case, it is difficult to see why Luce insists that Berkeley held a view – that we perceive what God "perceives" – which is not only incompatible with Berkeley's own assertions, but one which would strike Berkeley as repugnant to reason. As a matter of fact, there is strong evidence that Berkeley would deny that

God "perceives" IDEAS or anything at all. Though, to be sure, Berkeley often seems to suggest that God perceives what is not perceived by a finite perceiver or finite perceivers, his considered opinion seems to be that God WILLS the sense-data we experience and knows – or contains in His understanding – all things. If an appeal may be made to the authority of the *Siris*, Berkeley surely may be said to have repudiated the notion that God perceives anything at all. Berkeley emphatically says that

> There is no sense nor sensory, nor anything like sense or sensory, in God. Sense implies . . . and denotes a dependence in the soul which hath it. Sense is a passion . . . God knoweth all things, as pure mind or intellect; but nothing by sense, nor in nor through a sensory.[28]

It would seem, at any rate, that Berkeley's thought was moving in the direction of an awareness of the need to distinguish between the phenomena apprehended by finite beings and the eternal IDEAS in the divine mind. Thus, in the *Dialogues between Hylas and Philonous*, Philonous [Berkeley] asserts the following:

> Do I not acknowledge a twofold state of things – the one ectypal or natural, the other archetypal and eternal? The former . . . created in time; the latter existed from everlasting in the mind of God.[29]

There can be little doubt that, no matter how many difficulties such a view may engender, Berkeley's considered position, in this regard, is that we do not perceive (or apprehend in perception) that which God is cognizant of or that which is in God's mind. It would seem that the sensible object or thing (i.e., collection of ideas), X, which a finite individual perceives cannot be said to be the SAME thing, X, when it is not perceived by a finite percipient since the being of that X in the mind of God is surely distinct from the being of such an entity in relation to a finite perceiver. Now, it is precisely this difficulty which necessarily arises in an analysis of Berkeley's theory of perception. That is, the difficulty concerning the identity of the perceived or perceivable entity.

E. The Problem of Identity

The problem of the identity of objects or sense-ideas could be approached from two fundamental directions. On the one hand, there is the problem discussed above – that is, whether that which is perceived by a finite percipient (or by finite percipients) bears any relationship to what is "in the mind of God". On the other hand, it may be asked whether finite individuals perceive the SAME thing. This latter question is one which must be examined in order to clarify the implications of Berkeley's analysis of perception.

Berkeley tends to affirm, in regard to this question of identity, that if we take the word SAME to mean what it ordinarily means, then it may be admitted that different observers may be said to perceive the same thing or that the same thing "exists" for different perceivers. Berkeley assumes that the word "same" is ordinarily used to refer to those conditions under which no distinction or variety is perceived. That is, we apply the term SAME to that which cannot be distinguished from something else. In this sense, Berkeley admits that the "same thing" can be perceived by, and exist "in the minds" of, different percipients.

Generally speaking, however, Berkeley tends to attack the notion of identity as an abstraction. He invariably attempts to reduce all sameness to similarity. It would seem to be obvious, however, that even in ordinary usage we do not mean that someone (or some group of percipients) perceived a similar object, thing, or idea, when we say that he (or they) perceived the SAME object, thing, or sense-datum. Ordinarily, when we say that X is similar to Y we mean that X resembles Y or is "like" Y; we do not seem to mean that X is the same as Y. Now, it has been observed by A. A. Luce that Berkeley argues for what he calls "virtual identity" – that is, close similarity.[30] Undoubtedly, this is Berkeley's considered opinion. But it must be noted that Berkeley's assertion that this entire difficulty is simply a dispute about a word[31] is surely false. For, it is precisely his rather offhand discussion of the problem of identity which seems to lead Berkeley into serious difficulties.

Ultimately, Berkeley seemed to believe that the problem of identity was solved by an appeal to God's knowledge of "things", since a natural object or thing would possess literal identity in God alone. Berkeley claims that if several men were affected in the same way by sense-data (assuming that they are endowed with efficiently functioning sense organs), they would " . . . agree in their perceptions".[32] He goes on to say that those percipients who were attentive to the uniformity of what was perceived would describe what they had perceived as the same thing. Those, on the other hand, who were attentive to the fact that there were a diversity of perceivers would undoubtedly aver that DIFFERENT things had been perceived. In effect, Berkeley seems to imply that there is no serious distinction between these two ways of explaining the perceptions of several individuals.

Now, it would seem that, in accordance with Berkeley's statements, we would have to assume that if twenty men were looking at, say, the moon, they each would perceive certain sense-data which would be mind-dependent. But the collection of sense-data they would identify as THE MOON would be numerically distinct for each perceiver. It would be erroneous to assert that each of the twenty percipients would be perceiving the "same" moon. Rather, each perceiver is apprehending something which is SIMILAR to what the others are perceiving. The implications of Berkeley's discussion (particularly in the *Dialogues*) seem to be that it must be possible to refer the sensations of various perceivers to an identical object which, accordingly, must be something other than the particular and specific sensory data of different percipients. It is obvious, then, that if all things are nothing but sense-data (i.e., collections of sense-data) and if, in addition, the receptivity of such data requires the subjective modifications of the individual percipient, then it follows that no two persons can perceive THE SAME THING at all. Ultimately, then, it is God who causes the individual percipients to be affected by similar but not identical sensory phenomena.

Thus, if perceiver one, P_1, and perceiver two, P_2, "look at", let us say, a house, God causes similar sense-data to be apprehended by each perceiver. If P_1 and P_2 are asked to report what they have perceived, they can explain what they have perceived only in terms of the "images" which have been preserved in their memories. By describing the images which they have recalled the percipients will be able to compare these images and recognize the similarity between the two sets of images. Hence, they may infer that they have perceived a similar thing, say, a house. In accordance with Berkeley's position, they could not legitimately assert that they had perceived the SAME house. To paraphrase Berkeley's statement in the *Dialogues between Hylas and Philonous*, we may say that the "real" house which exists outside the consciousness of the percipients is truly known and comprehended by the infinite mind of God alone.[33] Now, if the "real" thing is said to exist in the mind of God, then it is obvious that finite perceivers do not perceive the REAL thing at all. Berkeley has recourse to his notion of archetypes in the mind of God (which, he claims, are external to finite minds) in order that the "ends of identity" are served. The being of the perceived, then, is only a relative mode of being since things (collections of sense-data) have an eternal, absolute existence in the divine mind. It seems, then, that the notion that, for Berkeley, " . . . things appear to be what they are, and are what they appear to be . . . "[34] turns out to be quite doubtful. What finite percipients apprehend in sense-experience must be, according to Berkeley's essential position, the phenomenal manifestations of the eternal archetypes in the mind of God.

In order to indicate the phenomenalistic character of Berkeley's analysis of perception, it will be necessary to deal with his conception of objects or things, with the process he described as mediate perception, and the inchoate formulation of a constructionist theory of objects. In addition, I will attempt to indicate the direction which he seems to adopt in his treatment of the nature of perception in general in the *Siris* (Appendix A).

Notes

1 *Vide*: A. A. Luce, *Berkeley's Immaterialism* (London, 1950), p. 39; and E. A. Sillem, *George Berkeley and the Proofs for the Existence of God* (London, 1957), p. 100.

2 Berkeley, *De Motu*, Section 53.

3 Berkeley, *Principles* . . . , Section 2.

4 *Ibid*., Section 5.

5 *Ibid*., Section 4.

6 John Locke, *Essay Concerning Human Understanding*, I, ii, xxiii.

7 Vide: D. M. Armstrong, *Perception and the Physical World* (New York, 1961), p. 3ff.

8 D. M. Armstrong, *op. cit*., p. 6.

9 Berkeley, *Principles* . . . , Section 18.

10 *Cp*. A. Joussain, *Exposé critique de la philosophie de Berkeley* (Paris, 1921), p. 46: "Le monde sensible n'est qu'un ensemble de perceptions, mais ces perceptions s'imposent à nous: elles sont involontaires . . . "

11 Berkeley, *op. cit*., Section 26.

12 *Cp*. A. Joussain, op. cit., p. 46: "Toute cause est active, et nous ne pouvons concevoir une activité différente de notre volonté . . . Si donc il existe hors du nous une cause productrice de nos perceptions, c'est qu'il existe hors du nous un être qui veut les perceptions en nous."

13 Berkeley, *op. cit*., Section 30.

14 *Ibid*., Section 18.

15 *Ibid*., Section 33.

16 Berkeley, *op. cit*., Section 139.

17 John Wild, *George Berkeley* (London, 1936), p. 175.

18 Berkeley, *T.V.V.E.*, Section 12.

19 G.A. Johnston, "The Relation between Collier and Berkeley", *Archiv für Geschischte der Philosophie*, XXV, 168.

20 George Berkeley, "Three Dialogues between Hylas and Philonous", in Mary W. Calkins, ed., *Berkeley: Selections* (New York, 1929), II, p. 280. This work will be subsequently cited as *D.H.P.*

21 *Ibid.*, p. 278.

22 *Ibid.*, I, p. 56.

23 *Cf.* J. M. Hone and M. M. Rossi, *Bishop Berkeley* (London, 1931), p. 68.

24 A. A. Luce, "Berkeley's Doctrine of the Perceivable", *Hermathena*, LX, 14.
25 *Ibid.*, p. 15.

26 George Berkeley, *Commonplace Book*, in A. A. Luce and T. E. Jessop, eds., *The Works of George Berkeley* . . . , I, pp. 69, 96.

27 Berkeley, *D.H.P.*, II, p. 279.

28 Berkeley, *Siris*, Section 289.

29 Berkeley, *D.H.P.*, III, p. 332.

30 A. A. Luce, *op. cit.*, p. 15.

31 Berkeley, *D.H.P.*, III, p. 323.

32 *Ibid.*

33 *Ibid.*, III, pp. 305-306.

34 A. A. Luce, "Berkeley's Search for Truth", *Hermathena*, LXXXII, 15.

III

Ideas and Things

> We not only impose on others but often on ourselves, by the unsteady or ambiguous use of terms.
> Bishop Berkeley, *The Theory of Vision Vindicated and Explained.*

Although Berkeley was certainly aware of the deceptive characteristics of language and was intent upon clarity of expression, it is obvious that it is precisely the ambiguous use of the term "idea" which has led to a good deal of the misinterpretation of Berkeley's thought. The conception of "idea", in Berkeley's writings, often seems to adopt as many disguises as Proteus. It is for this reason that an attempt will be made to determine the various ways in which Berkeley uses this conception in the explication of his theory of perception. An attempt will be made to determine the way in which Berkeley uses the term in his earlier works and, in an appendix to this chapter, the conception of "idea" in the *Siris* will be examined. Because of the manifest change of emphasis in regard to the relationship between sensation and knowledge, and the consequent mutation of the conception of idea, in Berkeley's *Siris*, a brief analysis of that work would seem to be appropriate.

In his *Essay towards a New Theory of Vision* Berkeley describes an idea as " . . . an immediate object of sense, or understanding".[1] An idea, Berkeley repeatedly insists, is that which is immediately perceived. It is the atomic element apprehended in the perceptual process. How does this conception of idea differ from that of John Locke? It appears that the most basic and essential difference would be that, for Locke, an idea has a representative function. In addition, Locke's conception of idea is, if anything, broader and more general than Berkeley's. In his *Essay on the Human Understanding* Locke explains that an idea is " . . . that term which . . . serves best to stand for whatsoever is the object of the understanding when a man thinks . . . "[2] He further explains that he uses this term to describe phantasms, notions, or species. In a letter written in defense of his position Locke asserted that " . . . the thing signified by "ideas" is nothing but the immediate objects of our minds in thinking".[3] In regard to the "simple ideas of diverse senses", Locke believed that the understanding is passively receptive to them in so far as " . . . the objects of our senses . . . obtrude their particular ideas upon our minds, whether we will or no . . ."[4] In this respect, it would seem that Berkeley's conception of the way in which sense-data are perceived does not differ significantly from Locke's position. There is, however, a major and essential difference between Locke's conception of ideas and Berkeley's which is obvious in the following passage from the *Essay on the Human Understanding*:

> Whatever the mind perceives in itself or is the immediate object of perception, thought or understanding, that I call an idea; and the power to produce any idea in our mind I call quality of the subject wherein that power is . . . the powers to produce . . . ideas in us . . . I call "qualities" . . .[5]

Now, there can be no doubt that Berkeley, unlike Locke, tends to incorporate both the ostensible qualities of things and sensations under the rubric "idea". In addition, of course, Berkeley does not attribute any causal "power" to things or qualities. Furthermore, Locke conceives of an idea which has reference to a primary quality as having a representative function. Locke believes, of course, that the primary or original qualities are inseparable from bodies and have the capacity or power to, as it were, "produce" simple ideas in us.

At any rate, in his *Essay towards a New Theory of Vision* Berkeley refers to ideas as (a) objects of sense which are immediately perceived and (b) objects of the understanding. Berkeley adds, in the *Theory of Vision Vindicated and Explained*, that all of the objects of all the particular senses may become objects of imagination in so far as the imagination has the power to represent sensible things.[6] The objects of sense or sense-ideas do not seem to have, for Berkeley, any representative function. In his *Commonplace Book* the youthful Berkeley makes a point of insisting that " . . . the referring ideas to things which are not ideas . . . is one great cause of mistake . . . "[7] The ideas of sense do not represent something "beyond" themselves. The immediate perception of sense-data is not the perception of images of, or copies of, something else. It is simply the apprehension of the sensible data themselves. Berkeley tended to argue that the conception of an object which cannot be immediately perceived is illogical.

Of course, it may be said that there is one sense in which an element of representationalism cannot be evaded. That is, the word "idea" is not, strictly speaking, identical with that to which it refers. For example, it cannot be said that the visual sense-data which Berkeley refers to in his *Essay towards a New Theory of Vision* are the same as that which is actually perceived. That is, the symbolic function of language incorporates, as it were, an element of representationalism into any theory of perception or theory of knowledge. The identification of a perceptual process requires, it would seem, the conceptual labeling of that process; but the term which identifies a process (or an aspect of a process) cannot be identical with that process. Thus, to designate an object or thing as "hard" seems to require some form of interpretation of the sensuous experience itself. In this respect, then, terms like "idea" do represent something which is other than themselves.

It is interesting to note, at any rate, that the ambiguity of the term idea was apparently directly incorporated into the conception by Berkeley himself. Thus, for example, he asserts, in one of the *Dialogues between Hylas and Philonous*, that " . . . My reason for using it [the word idea] was, because a necessary relation to the mind is understood to be implied by that term".[8] It would appear that it is precisely for this reason that Berkeley should have refrained from using the term "idea" in the way in which he did use it. It is apparent that Warnock's assertion that " . . . Berkeley's use of the term "idea" is NOT a use generally established in ordinary discourse"[9] is not quite accurate. For, it appears that Berkeley desired to include in the conception of idea the commonsense usage which implies an "existence in the mind". That is, Berkeley is not excluding the meaning of idea as a thought or conception which is an "object" of the understanding. To be sure, Berkeley does not restrict the term idea to such a specific meaning. But Berkeley is, in a sense, deliberately endeavoring to retain the ordinary usage of the word idea in order that it might serve as a prolepsis of his fundamental dictum that ideas exist for the mind or are mind-dependent.

Nevertheless, Berkeley describes IDEAS (visual sense-data, tactile sense-data) as both sensible qualities and sensations. He does not make any clear distinction between the sensible qualities of things and our sense-impressions of these qualities. The term idea includes, then, (a) an object of thought in general; (b) a sensible quality; (c) a sensation, and (d) an image (i.e., an "idea" of imagination). Now, at this point in our discussion we will be concerned primarily with the seeming confusion in Berkeley's writings between sensible qualities perceived and the sensations which are experienced by a percipient. G. E. Moore has clearly emphasized this difficulty in Berkeley's analysis of perception. Moore avers, quite rightly, that the term sensation is often misleading since there is a tendency for us to use such a term for the quality (say, the color green) which is perceived or "seen" and for the experience of the perception of that quality. As Moore put it:

> . . . when you are reading any philosopher who is talking about sensations (or about sense-*impressions* or *ideas* either), you need to look very carefully to see which of the two he is talking about in any particular passage – whether of the sense-data themselves or of our apprehension of them . . . [10]

Now, there is no doubt that Berkeley does, in fact, tend to fuse sense-data (qualities) with sensations. Moore, however, insists that we must carefully distinguish between the awareness of sensations and what is being perceived or sensed. Clearly, Moore's critique of Berkeley's account of perception raises some interesting questions. Moore attributes the "striking results" of Berkeley's analysis to the fact " . . . that *esse* is held to be *percipi*, solely because *what is experienced* is held to be identical *with the experience of it*".[11] Though Moore's objections appear to undermine Berkeley's position, it is interesting to note that he implies that Berkeley CONFUSED qualities and sensations or sense-data and our awareness of them. It would appear, in fact, that Berkeley did not confuse the two. He simply incorporated into the meaning of "idea" both the sensible quality perceived and the sensation experienced. Berkeley openly admits that what are designated as qualities are "imprinted" on our senses by a supra-finite spirit. He asserts, however, that sensible qualities and sensations are both experienced by a percipient being. Berkeley seems to believe that to speak of qualities or of sensations is simply to refer to two aspects of a single process. There is, Berkeley seems to be saying, a simultaneity between the experience of the quality and the experience of the sensation.

To say, as Moore does, that " . . . a sensation is, in reality, a case of "knowing" or "being aware of" or "experiencing" something",[12] would be to prejudice the case against Berkeley. Because, for Berkeley, this awareness of a sensation — this "reflection upon" a sensation — would be an act of memory or imagination. The discrimination between what is experienced and the experience of it is not "present" in or "discovered" in what Berkeley describes as "immediate perception". The point of Berkeley's discussion concerning the perception of intense heat in the *Dialogues* is, it would seem, simply that the pain and the intense heat are both perceived immediately or simultaneously, that is, as a matter of concrete experience, we do not discriminate between what is experienced and the experience of it.[13] Berkeley selects the sensible quality of heat in his illustration because it is a convincing illustration of the intimate relationship which exists between a sensible quality and a sensation. He is intent upon attempting to demonstrate that sensations and sensible qualities have one thing in common: they are both mind-dependent. In effect, Berkeley attempts to demonstrate that sensible qualities and sensations are both immediately perceived (and, hence, are IDEAS by definition).[14] In addition, of course, Berkeley desires to emphasize the mind-dependent status of both sensible qualities and sensations insofar as both are experienced by a percipient being who is "affected" by them.

A. Immediate Perception

It would appear that much of Moore's criticism of Berkeley presupposes a distinction which Berkeley himself was either unwilling or unable to make. The antagonism between the two viewpoints seems to revolve about a radical difference between Berkeley's analysis and interpretation of the nature of perception and Moore's implicit assumptions about the perceptual process. Perhaps an examination of a graphic illustration of Berkeley's analysis of perception may be helpful in demonstrating exactly how Berkeley understands what he means by "immediate perception".

In the third of the *Dialogues between Hylas and Philonous* there is an interesting discussion about the process of immediate perception. In discussing one of the classical illustrations of the argument from illusion – the bent or crooked appearance of an oar under water – Berkeley asserts that it is obvious that what is immediately perceived is precisely a "crooked oar". (Berkeley's considered opinion, of course, would be that what we call a crooked oar is actually a "collection of ideas" which have been immediately perceived.) The perceiver, he asserts, is not mistaken in regard to the particular data he actually perceives. The error arises in such perceptual situations only when the perceiver makes an INFERENCE from what has been immediately perceived. Inference is, of course, used in a psychological sense and not in a logical one. Now, according to Berkeley, if the perceiver would

> conclude that upon taking the oar out of the water he shall perceive the same crookedness; or that it would affect his touch as crooked things are wont to do; in that he is mistaken . . . his mistake lies not in what he perceives immediately, and at present (it being a manifest contradiction to suppose he should

err in respect of that) but in the wrong judgment he makes concerning the ideas he apprehends to be connected with those immediately perceived.[15]

Berkeley argues that there is no inference in immediate perception, there is simply the perceptual apprehension of the phenomenal object (i.e., collection of sense-data). The indubitability of immediate perception is one of the essential aspects of Berkeley's theory of perception. He does not admit that minimal kind of discrimination which would be required in order to identify a percept as real or illusory. That is, Berkeley assumes that there is no judgment made in immediate experience. Nor does he admit the distinction between what is experienced and the experience of it, the distinction which G. E. Moore assumes is present in immediate perception. For Berkeley, the perceptual process is characterized as the immediate perception of sense-data which are not distinguished from the experience of them. Berkeley tends to believe that any assertion made about WHAT is perceived already involves a reflection upon immediate experience or perception itself and is, hence, a cognitive activity, a reflection upon what has been experienced, a RECOLLECTION of an immediate experience and not the immediate experience itself. If someone is asked to say what he is perceiving — what he is experiencing — it seems that he must then reflect upon what is (or has been) experienced, he must provide an interpretation or judgment about the immediate experience itself.

The immediate perception of sense-data is, for Berkeley, the foundation of all perception. Precisely because he insists upon the immediate perception of "ideas of sense" as a non-inferential process it is not possible for him to admit, in the perceptual process itself, a distinction between the so-called quality which is experienced and the perceptual experience itself. The perception of sense-data is, as we have seen, a PASSION, in so far as sense-data are thought of as being "imprinted" on our sense-organs. To be sure, sensations are not what we touch or hear or see; they are what we HAVE or experience when we touch, hear or see something. But the point is that Berkeley has simply defined IDEAS as that which we immediately perceive and has incorporated into this definition what we designate as sensible qualities and sensations. There is little doubt that Berkeley tended to fuse perception and sensation. But the precise point of his arguments concerning primary and secondary qualities was to show that, ultimately, what we call "sensory or sensible qualities" are as intimately related to a percipient as are sensations. That is, sensible qualities are as "mind-dependent" as are sensations. And, since sense-qualities and sensations are both related to consciousness, they are, according to Berkeley, included under the conception of idea. It is argued that sensations are obviously related to consciousness since a subject or conscious being experiences them. The same is true of sensible qualities as well.

A criticism offered by Thomas Reid[16] may be helpful in attempting to understand Berkeley's position. Reid argues that it is certainly true that when, say, we prick our finger, we experience a sensation. But, even though the pin has length, figure, weight, etc., it bears no relation to a sensation. The pin, then, is an "object of sense", but not a sensation. To be sure, Berkeley would probably admit that a pin is clearly not a sensation. A pin or, for that matter, any "thing" at all is a "collection of ideas". Objects are, for Berkeley, the summation of their qualities (or sense-ideas). The pin, in Reid's illustration, and the sensation experienced are both "ideas" in Berkeley's sense of the word. The sensation of pain is an "idea" and the pin is a "collection of ideas". Sense-qualities and sensations both bear an intimate relationship to a perceiver. Although we may speak about sense-qualities and sensations as distinct, Berkeley seems to argue, they, nevertheless, share one characteristic in common: an obvious relation to a percipient being. Berkeley seems to argue that we "have" sensations and sense-qualities in so far as we are passively receptive to both perceptual phenomena. And he tends to equate the "having" of a sense-datum with perception in general. Berkeley uses the term "idea", as we have seen, precisely because it indicates a relation to a consciousness. Whatever is immediately perceived (whether it be a sensation or a percept) is an "idea". And what is immediately perceived has, obviously, an intimate relationship to a percipient being. Berkeley avers that an "idea" can also be represented in imagination. Whatever can be represented in imagination is an "idea". Hence, if we can imagine a sensation or a sensible quality, then both the sensation and the quality are "ideas" according to this criterion.

Although Berkeley originally incorporated into the conception of IDEA the immediate objects of understanding, he later modified his conception in order to exclude such a meaning. Objects of the understanding were, in the *Principles*, described as NOTIONS. In the *Siris* Berkeley further distinguished between sense-ideas or image-ideas by asserting that the activity of thought or reasoning provides us with a new and distinct class of objects – *entia rationis* – from which, in turn, notions and principles are formed.[17]

The characteristic function of perception for Berkeley is the apprehension of elementary sensory data which are immediately perceived. IDEAS are dependent upon the mental acts of perceiving, imagining, and willing. The finite percipient, in addition, is passively receptive to the sense-data which are caused by the divine will. Though Berkeley tends occasionally to speak of perception as essentially an activity, his considered opinion seems to be that in volition alone is the mind truly active. The mode of being of the *percipi* is, of course, entirely distinct from the mode of being of the perceiver. The mind, being fundamentally distinct from its "ideas", is the unchanging unity "supporting" them. The self or mind is, for Berkeley, a thinking, active principle which "operates" upon "ideas". There is no doubt that Berkeley tended to argue from the perception of a concatenation of sense-data to the underlying, self-identical unity which perceives the multiplicity of phenomena. Thus, for example, in the third of the *Dialogues between Hylas and Philonous*, Berkeley asserts that

> I know that I, one and the same self, perceive both colours and sounds . . . I am . . . one individual principle, distinct from colour and sound; and . . . from all other sensible things and inert ideas . . . I know . . . that a spirit knows and perceives ideas.[18]

At any rate, a sense-datum may be described as that which is immediately present to the mind before it has been elaborated by inference, interpretation, or construction. Although Berkeley occasionally asserts that the terms "thing" and "idea" are more or less equivalent, he also describes a thing as a "collection of ideas". He claims that he is not for changing what we call things into ideas, but he intends, rather, to change ideas into things. Now, it would seem rather odd that Berkeley should insist on this point since he has often affirmed that all the things of our experience are nothing apart from a cluster of ideas "in the mind". It would appear, then, that Berkeley has, in fact, CHANGED things into ideas. In order to understand why this is so, we must turn next to another important aspect of Berkeley's theory of perception, that of mediate perception.

B. Mediate Perception

Berkeley's conception of the nature of mediate perception seems to have an apparent relationship to the phenomenalistic view that things are constructions out of sense-data (ideas) and, for that reason, it should be examined with some care. The function of mediate perception is primarily to enable us to anticipate possible perceptions. "Ideas" are the immediate objects of sense-experience which function as signs of phenomena which might be perceived. There would seem to be some difficulty in Berkeley's explication of mediate perception. For, as we have seen, he has insisted that what is immediately perceived is indubitable. Berkeley would probably have agreed with Russell's assertion that

> There are in fact no illusions of the senses, but only mistakes in interpreting sensational data as signs of things other than themselves.[19]

Berkeley introduces mediate perception in order to indicate the process by which what is immediately perceived "suggests to the mind" possible perceptions.

The question that may be raised in regard to mediate perception is, by what "aspect" of the mind is such perception carried out? It seems that if no "idea" is apprehended by us simply as such but as signifying something which is other than itself, then the immediate apprehension of a sense-idea and the apprehension of its sign-function are two aspects of one specific perceptual process. If this is the case, then it is apparent that perception itself must involve or entail the powers of discriminating and relating, capacities which Berkeley tends to relegate to thinking or judging. Though Berkeley had, in his *Essay towards a New Theory of Vision*, attributed what he later described as mediate perception to an act of the understanding,[20] he tends (at least in his *Dialogues between Hylas and Philonous*) to attribute the same activity to (mediate) perception. But this anticipation of experience seems to require some representation of possible perceptions. The following illustration may make this point clearer. If an individual immediately perceives that visible appearance which he has learned to identify as a "wall", and if this perceiver then anticipates how this "wall" would "feel" if he walked up to it and touched it, we must assume that he is IMAGINING what his possible perceptions will be. To be sure, his imagination of a possible sense-experience is guided by, or determined by, his previous experiences of such phenomenal appearances. But, nevertheless, imagination plays a significant function in the anticipation of experience. The phenomena signified by the data which are immediately perceived are not (at the moment at which the sign-ideas are perceived) "ideas" of SENSE. What, then, are these signified phenomena?

Since Berkeley has made a point of asserting that the process of suggestion is an act of mediate perception, it may be assumed that Berkeley does not intend to attribute the entire process to acts of the understanding, acts of judgment or inference. If this is the case, then the phenomena signified in mediate perception must be "ideas" of the IMAGINATION. The signified phenomena may be grouped in the third class of "objects of knowledge" which Berkeley mentions in the *Principles*:

> ideas formed by . . . memory and imagination . . . representing those originally perceived.[21]

The signified data are, then, represented in imagination; they are "creations" of the will of the finite perceiver. Images, Berkeley claims, copy and represent something other than themselves. The immediate perception of certain sounds, for example, leads us to imagine that there is a coach approaching. From the basic and immediate perception of only some of the perceptual data out of which a "coach" is constructed, we reconstruct (in imagination) the other sense-phenomena we assume we would perceive if we had seen and touched what we imagine to be a coach. Thus, though the objects of imagination may be, as Berkeley says, less orderly, coherent, steady than sense-ideas they, nevertheless, play a significant function in his theory of perception.

It is interesting to note that even in regard to Berkeley's notion that things are collections of ideas, it would appear that the imagination (one is tempted to say the "productive imagination") plays a significant role. For, as we have seen, the sense-contents out of which a thing may be "constructed" are actually inexhaustible. Hence, the act of "joining together" the various sensory data may not be, as we have suggested, a formal cognitive process (a LOGICAL construction), but an IMAGINATIVE construction or "reproduction". Perhaps the various sense-ideas are "collected" by what Kant described as that " . . . blind though indispensable function of the mind", the imagination. The synthetic activity of uniting the elements of perception – the data immediately perceived and the sensory data mediately perceived – into one specific thing may very well be, for Berkeley, an act of imagination and, hence, an act of the will. Whether this is the case or not, it seems that the imagination is a necessary ingredient of perception.

Although we have seen that Berkeley insists that things are collections of ideas, he does not seem to have explicated either the means or the method by which this "collection" is carried out. The various sense-data are given to us; they are not "constructs" of any kind. But perhaps "things" are indeed "constructs", though not logical constructs. That is, perhaps Berkeley's analysis of perception may be interpreted in such a way that the act of collection may be considered as a synthetic act of imagination (hence, act of the will) which mediates between the immediate data of sense-experience and the CONCEPTUAL INTERPRETATION of that data.

If a thing "comprises" not only actual presentations, but suggested or associated "re-presentations", it would appear that the representations (which must be imagined phenomena) do serve to contribute significantly to perception since these representations make up by far the larger part of what we take to be the sense-content of the perceptual apprehension. The only serious objection to such an interpretation of Berkeley's analysis of perception would seem to be his obvious tendency to derogate "ideas of imagination" as being faint, indistinct, inconstant, etc. But this objection may not be damaging to the assertions which we have made since there is no reason to believe that Berkeley would assume that the phenomena signified by sense-ideas are indubitable. The perceiver may certainly be in error in regard to the perceptions he anticipates on the basis of what he has perceived immediately. Thus, there is no doubt that certain visual sense-data do suggest "to the mind" certain possible tangible phenomena; but Berkeley has insisted that the connection between such visual and tactile data is not necessary, but arbitrary. The representations formed in consciousness through imagination would seem to be, for Berkeley, only probable guides for the anticipations of experience. There is, Berkeley tends to say, no necessary connection between the signs (immediately perceived) and the phenomena which are signified. Representation seems to require both memory and imagination. And there is no apparent reason to assume that such mental acts may not lead to error.

Whether this interpretation of Berkeley's conception of mediate perception is correct or not, it is, nevertheless, an attempt to account for an obviously phenomenalistic aspect of his theory of perception: possible perceptions.

At any rate, an attempt will be made to argue that, according to Berkeley's analysis of perception, a THING cannot legitimately be considered an immediate object of sense. The thing cannot be, *pace* Berkeley's occasional remarks, equivalent to a sense-idea.

C. The Notion of a Thing

In conventional language a thing may be described as an individual, distinguishable entity or object which is distinguished from a quality or the qualities of an object. For Berkeley, it would appear that a thing is a synthesis of perceived or perceivable sense-data. He repeatedly insists that we immediately perceive sense-ideas (qualities or sensations). The totality or unity we describe as a thing is an entity which is composed of sense-data and is, therefore, not identical with the sense-data themselves. A thing is the sum of its experienced sense-data. But a thing cannot, strictly speaking, be THE SAME AS the data out of which it is "constructed". In fact, it may be asked how, according to Berkeley's account of perception, we are able to "extract" from the fleeting panorama of sense-data a synthetic "product", a unified totality or a thing. The phenomena immediately apprehended seem to be simply juxtaposed in a "spatial field". The identification of a specific congeries of sense-data as a synthetic unity implies some cognitive process. The "thing" is not, for Berkeley, a datum. Hence, things cannot be said to be immediately perceived.

The mere perception of Idea A, Idea B, Idea C, and Idea D in contiguous relationship would not lead us, necessarily, to describe these sense-phenomena as "parts" of, or "aspects" of, one thing. The very act of "joining together" the various sensory data would tend to lead us to believe that some cognitive or imaginative activity must take place. The cognitive activity would perhaps involve reflection upon what has been immediately perceived. The imaginative activity might involve the representation in imagination of the sense-data immediately perceived in some specific relationship. It would seem that perceptual apprehension relates a percipient to a multiplicity of phenomenal presentations alone. The designation of one group of, or conglomeration of, these sense-phenomena as A THING is a selective process, an intentional act, which seems to transcend the process of perception itself.

From what has been said it is obvious that an object or thing does not consist merely of a congeries of sensory data which are perceived at any one moment. According to Berkeley's account of the matter, it is the habitual experience of the association of a specific group of sense-data which leads us to identify THIS particular collection of sense-data as a thing (say, an apple). A thing is, then, a collection of "aspects" or elementary sensory phenomena which the perceiver colligates. Now, if we have accurately described Berkeley's position, it would seem that no one perceiver could perceive ALL of the sense-data "included" in a thing at a given moment. The collection of sensory data which we designate as a thing can be only selectively apprehended in perception. In addition, it is obvious that for Berkeley no two perceivers can apprehend the same thing. In the case of objects which are judged to be "at a distance", and are perceived by the "same" percipient at certain specific positions in the line of approach to such objects, there would not be ONE thing perceived, but many SIMILAR things. That this is the case, and this is an accurate interpretation of Berkeley's account of perception, is indicated in the following passage:

> Sight . . . doth not . . . inform you that the visible object you immediately perceive exists at a distance, or will be perceived when you advance farther onward; there being a continued series of visible objects succeeding each other during the whole time of your approach.[22]

It is asserted quite clearly that the perceiver will apprehend "a series of visible objects" or "things" as he approaches the apparent object.

It is interesting to note that Berkeley sometimes claims that a thing is "immediately perceived".[23] But this notion surely conflicts with his repeated assertion that sense-data are the immediate objects of perception. It also seems to conflict with the belief that we identify specific things on the basis of past experiences. After having observed a certain taste, color, figure, smell or size to appear "together", we describe this collection of sense-data as one distinct thing (say, a lemon). It would appear, then, that the identification of a certain collection of sensory data as a distinct thing requires the functions of memory and imagination. We must be able to recall the particular association or conjunction of ideas experienced in the past and we must also retain the images ("ideas of imagination") of these immediate perceptions in consciousness. As several of these sense-data are observed to accompany each other, they then come to be designated by one name and described as one thing.[24]

Things, then, despite Berkeley's occasional remarks to the contrary, are not immediately perceived at all. The identification of a certain group of specific "qualities" or sense-data as ONE THING is ultimately based upon a recollection of past experiences. Since visual and tactile sense-data are heterogeneous, the relationship between these data (a relationship which is implied in the description of a certain collection of sense-ideas as a distinct thing) is, for the finite perceiver, merely arbitrary. The congeries of sensory data which we now call, for example, "an apple" is similar to that previously experienced collection of sense-data only because of the benevolence of God, who is thought to be the cause of the specific sense-phenomena apprehended through the senses of finite percipients. The identification and re-identification of sensible THINGS which are thought to be similar to what was previously experienced would seem to require a recognition of specific sensory data juxtaposed in a certain relationship. That is, from the perceptual apprehension of only SOME of the "qualities" of a thing, there is an anticipatory expectation of the sense-data which WOULD be perceived under certain particular conditions. Berkeley had attempted to explain this anticipatory phenomenon in his *Essay towards a New Theory of Vision* in terms of what he called "praenotions" which are acquired on the basis of past experiences. That is, on the basis of past perceptions of sense-data we tend to develop some preconceptions about the nature of common objects which determine our identification of a particular congeries of sense-data as a distinct thing. To be sure, Berkeley seems to drop all references to these hypothetical praenotions in his later writings. But it must be admitted that they did seem to serve a specific function in his analysis of perception. For, the subtle distinctions which are sometimes made between one collection of sense-data and another would indicate that some preconceptions "accompany" our perceptions.

D. Discrimination in Perception

That there is some form of discrimination of this kind in perception may be illustrated in the following way. If we perceive that congeries of sense-ideas which we designate as a "flag" (say, the Belgian flag) at one time, and, at another time, we perceive another collection of sense-ideas which we describe as a "flag" (say, the German flag), by what criteria do we distinguish between the two flags? In this specific illustration, the colors of the two flags are the same (black, yellow, and red). And, for the sake of this discussion we will assume that the size, figure, texture, etc., of the two flags are similar (according to Berkeley there is no such thing as complete identity). Now, it would seem that in perception alone we are able to achieve a rudimentary discrimination between flag A and flag B. The Belgian flag, for example, is composed of three vertical columns of colors (in the following order: black, yellow, and red). The German flag is composed of three horizontal bars of the following colors (in order): black, red, and yellow. Since Berkeley describes a thing as simply a collection of sense-data how would it be possible to discriminate between these two THINGS? For, Berkeley does not seem to say very much about the arrangement of, or relations of, the congeries of sense-ideas we designate as a specific thing. Thus, if we simply listed the various sense-data out of which the German and the Belgian flags are composed, we would have to admit that these two things (flags) are "virtually identical" or similar according to the criteria which Berkeley provides. But it is obvious that a discrimination between the two appearances – the "things" we would describe as the Belgian and the German flag – is apprehended in perception alone. It would seem, then, that the distinctions we make between thing A and thing B are, in some sense, already "present" in the perceptual process itself. This apparent discrimination in immediate perception would seem to undermine Berkeley's notion that there is no judgment or inference made in immediate perception. The two things we have referred to (the two flags) are similar (or may be considered so) in so far as an analysis of the sense-contents out of which the things are "constructed" does not elicit any sharp distinction between the two things. Thus, if Berkeley desires to exclude judgment or inference from the immediate perceptual process – and the references to the appearance of the "crooked oar" cited above do indicate such an exclusion – , it would seem that Berkeley's theory of perception is, perhaps, inadequate to explain the type of discrimination which has been illustrated above. Whether this is the case or not, it would appear that Berkeley was reluctant to include inference or judgment in immediate perception *per se* in order to "save the phenomena". He was concerned to describe perceptual phenomena as they are apprehended by a percipient in the pre-judgmental immediacy of sense-experience.

E. Things and Ideas

A sensible object is, according to Berkeley, nothing but " . . . sensations combined, blended, or . . . concreted together."[25] The various sensory data which we perceive are not apart from the thing or object which we describe. The sense-data are presented together in such a way that they cannot be considered – to borrow H. H. Price's phrase – as "belonging to" an object.[26] Berkeley argues that a thing is not something which is distinct from its "modes or accidents". Thus, to say that X is hard, round, extended, smooth, etc., does not involve the attribution of such "qualities" to something which is distinct from these sense-qualities. If it were possible to "remove" all of the qualities or sense-data from what we describe as a thing, there would be nothing remaining. Berkeley avoided using the word "thing" in lieu of "idea" because he believed that the term "thing" " . . . is generally supposed to denote somewhat existing without the mind."[27] A remark in the *Commonplace Book* indicates a more subtle reason for not equating thing with idea.[28] At any rate, the assertion cited above raises an interesting question, referred to previously, concerning the problem of determining whether the "thing" is GIVEN in perception or whether it is, as some of the phenomenalists claim, a logical construction out of sense-data.

As we have indicated, Berkeley contends that the sensory data which are perceived by finite minds are "imprinted" on the senses by God. And, at times, Berkeley tends to suggest that the phenomena apprehended in sense-experience are "copies" of the eternal archetypes in the divine consciousness. God, at any rate, is thought to be the efficient cause of the sense-phenomena apprehended by finite perceivers. The phenomenal world is an elaborate system of signs which are presented to a finite consciousness in an orderly concatenation. These signs are interpreted by, and colligated by, finite perceivers. Berkeley variously describes a congeries of sense-ideas as a "sensible body", "body", or "thing". It appears, however, that he is not completely consistent in his use of the term "thing". In one explication of the meaning of the word "thing" Berkeley equates it with "Being" and asserts that it

> . . . is the most general name of all; it comprehends under it two kinds entirely distinct and heterogeneous . . . which have nothing common but the name, to wit, *spirits* and *ideas*.[29]

It is certain that Berkeley would not want to assert that a spirit is merely a collection of sense-ideas. He has repeatedly insisted that "minds" and IDEAS are totally distinct. The former are characterized by their activity; the latter by their passivity. If the above assertion is taken seriously, it would appear that, for Berkeley, the "thinghood" of the mind is completely distinct from the thinghood of a collection of sense-ideas. There is a further – and perhaps more serious – difficulty which emerges out of the equation Berkeley makes between being and thing. For, he affirms that a material substance means nothing but the notion of "Being in general", which he characterizes as " . . . the most abstract and incomprehensible of all other . . . " notions.[30] But surely Berkeley does not intend simply to replace the phrase "material substance" with the term "thing". For, if this were his intention, then all of his attacks against material substance could be, with equal force, turned against his conception of a thing.

Despite the apparent terminological difficulties in which Berkeley is occasionally involved, he has distinguished between material substance and his conception of a thing. A material substance was thought to be that which existed unperceived as the "support" for various qualities. Now, it would seem that Berkeley's concept of THING does not refer to something "external" to the perceiver nor is it thought to be the SUPPORT of sensible qualities or sense-data. A thing is not some esoteric entity which is distinct from a specific collection or set of sensory phenomena.

It must be admitted, to be sure, that Berkeley has not provided a clear or detailed analysis of the way in which we "construct" things or bodies out of sense-contents. Berkeley's notion that things are congeries of sense-ideas is only barely analogical with the sophisticated process – derived from the philosophy of mathematics and suggested to Bertrand Russell by A. N. Whitehead – described as the method of logical construction.[31] But we may assume that Berkeley would probably have agreed with Russell's assertion that – in accordance with the principle of parsimony – a thing should not be distinguished from the elements out of which it is composed and should be considered as identical with these elements or appearances.[32]

Although it has sometimes been said that Berkeley did not ultimately deny that there are "material things", this view does not seem to receive any significant support from Berkeley's explicit assertions. Since we may safely assume that Berkeley took quite seriously his "doctrine of immaterialism", the phrase "material object" would appear to be, for him, a *contradictio in adjecto*. To be sure, it would be quite accurate to say that he did not deny that we have a conception of "sensible objects", "bodies", or "things". One thing is distinguished from another thing simply by the reflection upon the relationship which is perceived between the various sense-data. The judgment that A is one thing and that B is another thing depends upon a memory of past experiences. The anticipations of what WOULD be experienced if such and such actions were undertaken would require, as we have seen, some preconception of the nature of the specific data out of which a particular thing is "composed". It is obvious, of course, that the totality of the sense-data out of which a specific thing is said to be "composed" cannot be perceived by one finite being. The elements of a thing which are not directly or immediately perceived are "inferred" from what is immediately perceived. This anticipation of possible sense-experience is, of course, based upon a memory of past experiences of similar phenomena.

Now, in the particular case cited above — the perception of a "crooked oar" — it would seem that Berkeley insists that we actually perceive that collection of sense-ideas which we designate as a "crooked oar". And, at the same time, any inferences or judgments we make concerning the anticipated tactile sensations we would experience if we took the "oar" out of the water are, of course, liable to error. Perhaps Berkeley would say that we do not, in this instance, EXPECT to experience certain specific tactile sensations (e.g., that the oar would feel "crooked") simply because of our memory of the past experiences of such visual phenomena. The "crooked" oar and the "straight" oar would both be, according to Berkeley, sensible or phenomenal "objects". There is no contradiction, in Berkeley's thought, in asserting that a particular thing "feels" straight and yet "looks" (under certain conditions) crooked. For, he has repeatedly insisted that visual and tactile sense-data are completely heterogeneous.

Nevertheless, Berkeley seems to argue that from the immediate perception of SOME of the aspects or appearances of something we are able to designate that system of appearances as a specific thing. To be sure, he does not deny that our anticipated perceptions may be false. If, for example, we perceive that collection of sense-data which we designate — on the basis of recollection of past experiences of similar congeries of sense-data — as, say, a lemon, and we anticipate how this apparent "lemon" would taste if we were to bite into it, we could very well be in error. If, that is, this visual appearance, this "apparent" lemon, was, for example, a wax imitation of the fruit, then only further perceptual data (e.g., sensations of smell or taste) could aid us in the correction of the judgment made on the basis of what was immediately perceived by sight. Although one thing may be said, metaphorically, to "share" SOME of the sense-ideas (qualities) of another thing, it cannot be said to "share" ALL of the similar sense-data of another thing. And, according to Berkeley's conception of "virtual" identity, two things which "shared" the SAME sense-ideas would not be identical, but only similar. In fact, these two things would be said to be "composed" of similar (but not the same) sense-data.

At any rate, it is interesting to note that Berkeley tended to give to the imagination the function of the anticipation of possible perceptions. For, it would appear that the anticipation of, for example, the tactile perceptions of what appears to be a "wall", requires not only a memory of past experiences of such phenomena (associated with what is designated as a wall), but an imaginative "construction" of the sensations which would be perceived if we walked up to what we believe to be a wall and actually reached out and touched it. This entire discussion, however, seems to bring us back to the same difficulties which were encountered in an analysis of Berkeley's doctrine of suggestion. What is immediately perceived, according to him, functions as a SIGN of what might be perceived.[33] Thus, the immediate perception of sense-ideas A, B and C provides the percipient with signs or cues which are used in order to anticipate possible perceptions – say, the perceptions of data D, E, F, etc. There is no necessary connection between the various sense-phenomena which we think a specific thing is "composed of", nor is there any guarantee that the sense-data we perceive immediately are actually "related to" the sensory data which they "suggest" to our consciousness. In fact, a thing is, for a finite perceiver, an arbitrary collection of sense-data. Only the preconceptions retained in memory, which are derived from past experiences of a certain conglomeration of sense-data leads us to assume that what we are immediately perceiving is similar to that "thing" which we had previously perceived. We have learned, then, to recognize, to RE-COLLECT or identify a specific thing on the basis of the repeated experience of similars. The recollection or memory of certain sensory data in contiguous relationship leads us to expect certain other perceptions.

Although the expectations of experience are dependent upon memory, the anticipations of experience are dependent upon imaginative representation. For, Berkeley has asserted that imagination has the capacity to represent all SENSIBLE THINGS. At any rate, the notion of a thing actually contains more in it than what is perceived in any particular situation or at any particular time.[34] The conception of an object or thing involves the selective perceptual apprehension of the sense-data from a group or family of regularly interrelated and interconnected sensibilia which constitute a particular object or thing.

The fundamental feature of the notion of a phenomenal thing is its predictive function. In the course of ordinary perception we do not usually attempt to verify our anticipated perceptions. There is simply an assumption made concerning what would be experienced if certain actions were undertaken. The beliefs which may accompany our perceptions, however, are not themselves discovered or grounded in the nature of perception itself, but depend upon our memory of past experience. It is perhaps for this reason that Berkeley does not introduce the discrimination between veridical or "illusory" perceptions (e.g., in the case of the perception of the "crooked oar") into the perceptual process itself. In addition, of course, Berkeley also intends to preserve the indubitability of immediate perception. Nevertheless, as we have seen, the recollection of the past experience of such phenomenal entities as a "crooked oar" enables the percipient to avoid false judgments concerning the nature of possible perceptions. It is obvious, from the above discussion, that a THING is not immediately given in sense-perception. For, if a thing is thought to be a collection of immediate and mediate percepts, this implies the "presence" of an intentional activity – the act of collecting or colligating elements, aspects, or parts of what is presented to consciousness – which we may legitimately associate either with a cognitive mental act or a synthetic act of imagination.

Though Berkeley does not, of course, refer explicitly to a process resembling that of "logical construction", it is plain, from what has been said, that a THING is a synthetic unity, a "construct" which is formed by a conflation of specific sensory data apprehended by the various modalities of sense. The data immediately perceived by one modality of sense (say, vision) ultimately have a representative function in so far as they "stand for" or "signify" possible perceptions. The sense-data which are immediately perceived are SIGNS representing that which could be or may be perceived under certain specific conditions. As Berkeley puts it:

> From the ideas you actually perceive by sight, you have by experience learned to collect what other ideas you will . . . be affected with, after . . . a certain succession of time and motion.[35]

Ultimately, then, a "thing" cannot be thought of as "given" in sense-perception. The "existence" of a thing is derivative and ultimately must be expressed in terms of the more essential sense of the existence of elementary sensory data. Berkeley's analysis of perception leads him to embrace a position very similar to phenomenalistic theories of perception. This is especially the case in regard to his discussion of the anticipations of possible perceptions and to the notion that things can ultimately be reduced to collections of sense-data. The question concerning the explicit nature of Berkeley's relationship to the phenomenalistic theory of perception must be dealt with in order to understand the sense in which he may be described as a "species" of phenomenalist and to see why his own theoretical constructs led him to this interpretation of the perceptual process.

F. Appendix: Perception and Ideas in the *Siris*

Although an attempt has been made to examine Berkeley's conception of "ideas" specifically in reference to the process of perception, it may be fruitful to consider Berkeley's references to perception and "ideas" in the SIRIS. In his last major work Berkeley has produced a bewildering, bizarre chain of reasoning which wanders from a discussion of the virtues of tar water to the *Anima Mundi*! The Platonic or Neo-Platonic elements in this work seem to be a radical departure from Berkeley's earlier empiricism. Though some of the Platonic aspects of this work will be considered, a good deal of the material covered in the book will be "bracketed" and an attempt will be made to extract all references in the *Siris* which are directly concerned with the problem of perception.

In the *Siris* there is not only the rather negative aspect of Berkeley's general derogation of sense-perception, but the positive recognition that man is capable not only of perception but of cognition — the capacity to comprehend a distinct class of objects apart from sensible objects, i.e. entities of the mind — as well. Berkeley had never denied the possibility of the conception of universal notions though, to be sure, he launched a vitriolic attack against abstract ideas. In the "Introduction" to the *Principles* he explicitly avers that knowledge and demonstration are concerned with universal notions.[36] In addition, the entire discussion concerning the distinction between ideas and notions involves Berkeley's implicit acceptance of a mode of knowing distinct from knowledge derived from sense-experience. In *De Motu* Berkeley mentions that pure intellect, as distinguished from sense-perception and imagination, concerns itself with spiritual and unextended things.[37]

He admits, to be sure, that sensation does acquaint us with a multiplicity of appearances. But sense-perception *per se* is inadequate to apprehend CAUSES. The principles of science (e.g., the principle of causality) are not, obviously, objects of sense or imagination. They are, rather, "objects" of reason alone. Hence, the passive receptivity of sense is distinct from the spontaneous activity of thought. Berkeley asserts that truly to know something is to be able to interpret it and to describe what it signifies. Though we certainly perceive sounds, smells, tastes, etc., we cannot, strictly speaking, actually be said to understand them. To be sure, we are capable of thinking about sensation, of making inferences on the basis of what is immediately perceived. But the data apprehended in sense-perception are only the materials for cognition. As Berkeley puts it, " . . . strictly, the sense knows nothing."[38] Now, such a view is surely incompatible with the position which Berkeley puts forward in the *Principles* – viz. that the objects of KNOWLEDGE are "ideas of sense" or imagination. Nevertheless, Berkeley seems to have averted his attention (in the *Siris*) from the fleeting, impermanent, data perceived by sense and to have concentrated on the immovable and unchanging character of what he describes as "things intelligible".

Because of the mutability of the multiplicity of phenomena, such appearances cannot be considered as the ultimately real things. To be sure, Berkeley has often insisted that the sensible objects or bodies apprehended in sense-perception are "real" and are not simply illusions. But, as we have seen, the ideas of sense cannot be identical with the *Ideas* which have an eternal, immutable existence in the mind of God. Hence, they cannot be considered as ultimately real. One of the primal characteristics of true existents is that they be one and the same, i.e. self-identical. And it is obvious that, for Berkeley, "ideas" can only be LIKE other sense-ideas and the things which are "formed" out of the congeries of sense-data can only be similar to other such collections of sense-data.

Particular entities, then, can only be similar. It is perhaps for this reason that Berkeley introduced the archetypes "in the mind" of God. That is, only the IDEAS known by God can be said to possess complete "self-identity". As J. O. Wisdom has said, Berkeley believed that the problem of identity was solved by

> . . . the theocentric side of his philosophy, according to which a natural object possessed literal identity in God.[39]

In the ideas of sense and imagination there seems to be no unity prior to what Berkeley calls "acts of the mind". Thus, the process of the synthesis of the unity of the phenomenal ideas requires, as we have seen, an act of the mind, a cognitive process. In a passage in the *Siris* Berkeley says that sensible and imaginable things are " . . . in themselves aggregates, consisting of parts or compounded of elements",[40] and are, therefore, many. Such assertions are not incompatible with Berkeley's earlier position. We have seen that the process of uniting, combining, colligating sense-data requires some mode of cognition. Unity or oneness is not found in experience, but is a conception which incorporates, organizes and makes intelligible the manifold of sensory-ideas. It is quite remarkable how closely Berkeley comes to anticipating a Kantian attempt to reconcile the claims of rationalism and the claims of empiricism, to delineate clearly the relationship between perception and conception. He seems, at times, on the verge of describing unity as a "category of the understanding", a conception which "organizes" the multiplicity of sense-impressions.

Although Kant's analysis of the process of the synthetic unity of perceptual data is, to be sure, more thorough and more sophisticated than Berkeley's occasional flirtations with such a conception, there is little doubt that the direction of Berkeley's thought in this regard was leading him to a position resembling that of Kant. Here, for example, is Kant's account of the act of "connexion":

> All connexion whether or not we become conscious of it . . . is an act of the understanding which we might call by the general name of synthesis in order to indicate . . . that we cannot represent to ourselves as connected in the manifold anything which we have not, ourselves, previously connected.[41]

In addition, we may imagine that Berkeley would have welcomed the following distinction between perception and cognition which Kant epitomized in the assertion that:

> By means of sense objects are *given* to us and sense alone provides us with *perceptions*; by means of the understanding objects are *thought* and from it there arise concepts.[42]

Although no attempt is being made to equate Berkeley's position in the *Siris* with that of Kant, there would seem to be, as we have seen, some evidence that the Kantian analysis of perception and cognition was, in vague, seminal form, emerging in Berkeley's mature thought. The things which seem to ordinary consciousness most real – the sensible appearances – when exposed to the searchlight of reflection appear to be no more than "fleeting phantoms". Berkeley does not deny phenomenal being to the objects of sense in the *Siris*. But he asserts, now and again, that sense-perception has primarily a pragmatic function. It is by means of sense-perception that we are able to function adequately in regard to the practical matters of ordinary existence. Sense-perception, however, enables us to apprehend only the appearances of things, the fluctuating, mutable, impermanent manifestations or signs of an ultimate reality which, perhaps, utterly transcends the limits of finite consciousness.

Berkeley's interest in Platonism may not simply be the result of a quasi-sentimental appreciation of the aesthetic aspects of such a vision of the "truly real". In fact, it would seem that there is, perhaps, a way of reconciling the transcendentalism of the *Siris* with Berkeley's typical position. For, Berkeley has come to recognize the necessity of accepting the reality of the archetypes in the divine mind. There is no doubt that he had always asserted that the ultimate reality was mind. Perhaps, Berkeley seems to suggest, in this "cave" of ordinary experience we may be permitted, if we exert our minds, " . . . some imperfect glimpses of the Divine Ideas . . . "[43] It is quite possible that Berkeley has, as we have said, seen the necessity of propounding the eternal existence of the divine ideas which are the "absolute existents" which the fleeting, perishable ideas of sense "copy", "imitate", "represent", or "resemble". Such speculation is not completely without support in Berkeley's writings. We have already seen that, according to his account of the nature of sense-data, these phenomena cannot be identical with the ideas which exist in the divine mind. Surely the mode of being of IDEAS "in" a finite mind cannot be identical with the mode of being of the IDEAS in the divine mind. It is clear that Berkeley has, in the *Siris*, simply taken seriously the distinction which he had made between the archetypal ideas in the mind of God and the ectypal ideas in the mind of finite beings. Whatever may have been Berkeley's final philosophical position in this regard, there would seem to be some cogency in the notion that Berkeley's theory of perception could be considered as a form of what J. O. Wisdom has called "theocentric phenomenalism".[44] This is illustrated in the discussion of "Perception and Phenomena" which emphasized the distinctions between the sensory phenomena apprehended by finite percipients and the immutable eternal objects known (but not, as many commentators on Berkeley have said, PERCEIVED) by God. It is Berkeley's theism, surely, which leads him to formulate at least one aspect of his phenomenalism. This, however, is only half of the story, since his concept of mediate perception and his inchoate phenomenology of the perceptual process also led his analysis of perception to a phenomenalistic conclusion.

Notes

1 Berkeley, *E.N.T.V.*, Section 45.

2 John Locke, *Essay Concerning Human Understanding*, I, 1, i, 8.

3 John Locke, "Third Letter to the Bishop of Worcester", in *Essay Concerning Human Understanding*, I, p. 6.

4 John Locke, *op. cit.*, I, ii, i, 25.

5 *Ibid.*, I, ii, 8, 8.

6 Berkeley, *T.V.V.E.*, Section 10.

7 Berkeley, *Commonplace Book*, I, p. 80.

8 Berkeley, *D.H.P.*, III, pp. 235-236.

9 G. J. Warnock, *Berkeley*, p. 129.

10 George E. Moore, *Some Main Problems of Philosophy* (New York, 1962), p. 45.

11 George E. Moore, *Philosophical Studies* (Paterson, N. J., 1959), p. 19.

12 *Ibid.*, p. 24.

13 Berkeley, *D.H.P.*, I, p. 176 *et seq. Cp.* Walter T. Stace, *Theory of Knowledge and Existence* (Oxford, 1932), p. 73: " . . . the solitary mind cannot be aware of any distinction between the *esse* and the *percipi* of its presentation. It cannot, for example, draw any distinction between 'blue' and 'awareness of blue'." *Cp.* also: A. J. Ayer, *Language, Truth and Logic* (New York, n.d.), pp. 139-140: " . . . these acts of sensing, which realists reproach Berkeley for having ignored, appear to me to be completely inaccessible to any observation".

14 *Cp.* D. W. Hamlyn, *Sensation and Perception* (New York, 1961), p. 109: "It is possible to use the phrase 'immediately perceived' in such a way that the thesis that we immediately perceive only our ideas becomes true by definition; and in effect this is what Berkeley does."

15 Berkeley, *D.H.P.*, III, p. 238.

16 Thomas Reid, *Essays on the Intellectual Powers of Man* (London, 1941), p. 126.

17 Berkeley, *Siris*, Section 297.

18 Berkeley, *D.H.P.*, III, pp. 233-234.

19 Bertrand Russell, *Human Knowledge: Its Scope and Limits* (New York, 1948), p. 167.

20 Berkeley, *E.N.T.V.*, Section 17.

21 Berkeley, *Principles . . .*, Section 1.

22 Berkeley, *D.H.P.*, I, p. 201.

23 *Ibid.*, pp. 191, 201.

24 Berkeley, *Principles . . .*, Section 1.

25 *Ibid.*, Section 99.

26 H. H. Price, *Perception* (London, 1932), p. 177.

27 Berkeley, *op. cit.*, Section 39.

28 Berkeley, *Commonplace Book*, A. 872: "Dangerous to make Idea and Thing terms Convertible, that were the Way to prove spirits are Nothing".

29 Berkeley, *Principles . . .*, Section 89.

30 *Ibid.*, Section 17.

31 Bertrand Russell, *Mysticism and Logic* (New York, 1957), pp. 149-153.

32 Ernst Mach in his *The Science of Mechanics* (Chicago, 1902), also emphasizes the importance of the principle of economy in scientific theory and method.

33 Berkeley, *T.V.V.E.*, Section 39.

34 Since, according to Berkeley's analysis of perception, we can (or could) experience further IDEAS it appears that a thing is actually inexhaustible. Certainly, for Berkeley, not all of the various combinations of the aspects of a thing could be apprehended in perception by a single percipient. *Cp.* A. A. Luce, "Berkeley's Doctrine of the Perceivable", *Hermathena*, LX (November, 1942), 12: "Every *thing*, for Berkeley, must . . . contain some perceivable ideas because a man's powers of perception are limited, and no

one sentient at a given time can perceive all the ideas included in the thing. The 'collection', which is the thing, can only be selectively apprehended by man . . . "

35 Berkeley, *D.H.P.*, I, pp. 263-264.

36 Berkeley, *Principles* . . . , "Introduction", Section 15.

37 Berkeley, *De Motu*, Section 53.

38 Berkeley, *Siris*, Section 253.

39 John O. Wisdom, *The Unconscious Origin of Berkeley's Philosophy* (London, 1953), p. 23.

40 Berkeley, *Siris*, Section 355.

41 Immanuel Kant, *Critique of Pure Reason*, trans, Max Müller (London, 1907), p. 744.

42 *Ibid.*, p. 40.

43 Berkeley, *Siris*, Section 337.

44 John O. Wisdom, *op. cit.*, p. 21.

IV

Berkeley and Phenomenalism

. . . we in this mortal state are like men educated in Plato's cave, looking on shadows with our backs turned to the light.

Bishop Berkeley, *Siris*, 263

Although it has often been noted that contemporary phenomenalism may be described as "Berkeley without God", the nature of the relationship between Berkeley's theory of perception and that of phenomenalism has rarely been spelled out. Because a detailed analysis of phenomenalism would carry us far beyond the intention of this enquiry, an attempt will be made to indicate the essential conceptions of phenomenalism and to show how Berkeley's perceptual analysis is specifically related to one or more of the aspects of what we may describe as "traditional" phenomenalism.

Primarily, an attempt will be made to indicate the relationship between Berkeley's perceptual theory and the two major forms of phenomenalism, factual phenomenalism and linguistic phenomenalism. Closely related to these forms of phenomenalism, of course, is the sense-datum theory. Hence, certain aspects of this theory will be briefly examined, especially because of its association with Berkeley's analysis of perception.

A. Phenomenalism

Although it is certainly true that, as Wilfrid Sellars has recently said, there are " . . . a number of "phenomenalisms" . . . which are variations on a common theme",[1] there is at least this common theme which we may describe as traditional phenomenalism. Essentially, phenomenalism is a theory which argues that in perception we do not directly or immediately apprehend physical or material objects, but more elementary data which have been variously described as "ideas", "sensa", "impressions", or "sense-data". Although phenomenalists have provided different descriptions of these elementary data, they are generally in agreement with the view that the existence of these perceptual data is dependent upon the specific perceptual situation. Material objects, for the phenomenalist, are "constructions" out of actual and possible sense-data or sense-contents. The phenomenalist argues that although it is possible to doubt that we perceive "things" or material objects, we are unable to doubt that we hear sounds, see colors, etc. H. H. Price expresses this view in the following way:

> When I see a tomato there is much that I can doubt. I can doubt whether it is a tomato that I am seeing, and not a cleverly painted piece of wax. I can doubt whether there is any material thing there at all . . . perhaps I am . . . the victim of some hallucination. One thing however I cannot doubt: that there exists a red patch of a round and somewhat bulgy shape, standing out from a background of other colour patches, and having a certain visual depth, and that this whole field of colour is directly present to my consciousness.[2]

The indubitability of the immediate perception of sense-data is one of the cornerstones of phenomenalistic theories of perception. Sense-data are said to EXIST insofar as they are being perceived by an individual perceiver. In addition, sense-data are private to the individual perceiving them and no two individuals can perceive the same sense-data. Although severely critical of the sense-data theorists, Gilbert Ryle has pointed out that they are simply attempting to indicate the immediate objects of sense which our usual "preoccupation" with common objects prevents us from acknowledging.[3] Though it may be admitted that our ordinary language is structured in terms of physical object statements, it is believed that what we directly or immediately apprehend in sense-perception are more elementary or "atomic" perceptual data. In his discussion of sense-data G. E. Moore originally identified them with the color, size and shape of an object, but later asserted that the "patch" itself (in his illustration the appearance of a white envelope) is the sense-datum which HAS a certain size, color and shape.[4] This is a distinction which must be borne in mind when we attempt to indicate the relationship between Berkeley's perceptual analysis and the sense-datum theory. At any rate, it is generally held that sense-data are momentary, particular existents which ARE insofar as they are being sensed. In order to avoid the difficulty of referring to "unsensed sense-data", Bertrand Russell introduced the term sensibilia which refers to " . . . objects which have the same metaphysical and physical status as sense-data without necessarily being data to any mind".[5] In a phenomenalistic theory of perception, of course, sensibilia serve the function of possible sense-data. And physical objects are described as complexes of actual and possible sense-data.

Despite the fact that Ernst Mach had dissociated himself from what he called "Berkeleyanism", he puts forward, in the following quotation, a view reminiscent of Berkeley and characteristic of what we have described as traditional phenomenalism. He asserts that

> Thing, body, matter, are nothing apart from the combinations of the elements, — the colors, sounds, and so forth — nothing apart from their so-called attributes.[6]

If we substitute the term sense-data for "elements" in Mach's assertion, we have a succinct formulation of phenomenalistic reductionism. For Mach, sensations are not regarded as "symbols of things", but, rather, a thing is NOTHING BUT a mental symbol for a complex of sensations. Mach's reduction to sensations, however, is something which later phenomenalists have tried to avoid. For, if visual sense-data are colors which are directly perceived, they cannot also be, at the same time, color-sensations. Since the phenomenalist does not generally want to identify sense-data with sensations, he uses the term sense-data to refer to what is immediately present to perceptual awareness — colors, sounds, smells, etc. In Mach's phenomenalistic formulation, at any rate, we have a fundamental factual emphasis which is present in all rudimentary forms of phenomenalism. Any THING simply is nothing but so many experienced sensations. Mach does not seem to have said very much about an essential aspect of later phenomenalisms, that of possible perceptions.

According to Russell's early theory of perception a thing is a "system of aspects" perceived or a "set of momentary sense-data". In his hypothetical construction of the external world Russell maintained that while all of the "aspects" of a thing are real the thing is a logical construction out of the perceptual data themselves.[7] In what he described as a possible theory of the construction of the external world Russell had introduced methods and concepts which influenced not only Rudolf Carnap's early phenomenalistic work but the subsequent development of phenomenalism in general. In his *Problems of Philosophy*[8] he had emphasized that the ultimate empirical entities are sense-data which are the most undeniable entities of sense-experience. In addition, as we have seen, Russell regards "unsensed sensibilia" as entities which may be denoted in constructions and which are described as similar to, and continuous with, sense-data even though no one is perceptually aware of them. The influence of Russell's analysis is seen clearly in Carnap's constructionism and in the notion that the foundation upon which knowledge rests is the reduction of statements about physical objects to statements about phenomenal data or the basic elements which are immediate experiences in their individual unity.[9] There is an obvious relationship between Russell's application of the method of logical construction to the "philosophy of physics" (in which matter would be "exhibited" in terms of sense-data) and A. J. Ayer's assertion that " . . . the existence of a material thing is defined in terms of the actual and possible occurrence of the sense-contents which constitute it as a logical construction . . . "[10] Things, according to Ayer, are not simply collections of sense-data or sense-contents, but logical constructions out of them. Russell illustrates the method of logical construction by referring to the problem of irrational numbers. If irrationals " . . . were inferred as the supposed limits of series of rationals which had no rational limit", this process leaves the "existence of irrationals merely optative". Hence, an irrational number should be defined "as a certain class of ratios, thus constructing it logically be means of ratios" and avoiding the problem of defining an irrational number by means of an ambiguous inference from ratios.[11] Applied in more simple terms to the concept of a "thing", logical constructionism is a reductive method by which a thing is identified with the class of its appearances in accordance with an adopted principle of economy of thought. If a thing can conceivably be identified with the entire class of its appearances, Russell argues, then there is no necessity to introduce any unnecessary entities (e.g., "a substance or substratum underlying these appearances"). All in all, Russell's analysis is a sophisticated extension of Occam's principle: *Entia non sunt multiplicanda praeter necessitatem.*

Although H. H. Price's analysis of perception may be described as a form of constructionism, it is not a phenomenalistic theory of perception even though Price does tend to incorporate and modify some of the characteristics of phenomenalism. Price's form of constructionism does not deny the existence of material objects independent of perceivers. It is concerned, rather, with the way in which the complex object (what Price calls the "complete thing") is constructed from elementary data. Adopting the terminology common to phenomenalism, Price asserts that sense-data are what is immediately given in sense-experience. He adopts the term sense-datum because it is a neutral term which refers to something which is indubitable, if momentary, and which is the most fundamental element apprehended in sense-perception. Sense-data are, for Price, the source of our apprehension of material things. The sense-data with which we are directly acquainted are particular, non-substantial existents which may be said to be "for" minds insofar as they are presentations only to minds. For Price, sense-data are, unlike material objects, non-causal and private.[12] Although the sense-data actually perceived are few, Price believes that

> What the perceptually conscious subject takes for granted when he senses a particular visual or tactual sense-datum is that there now exists a material thing to which this sense-datum belongs . . . [13]

The "same" material object which persists through time has sense-data of various kinds which "belong" to it and which may be present to our senses in many different ways. In fact, the sense-data which belong to a material thing are inexhaustible since all of the "aspects" of a specific thing could not be apprehended in perception by one or more percipients. The evidence derived from sense-perception, according to Price, is sufficient enough for us to assume the existence of a material thing. The actual existence of a material thing cannot be KNOWN since the object is "absolutely determinate" and, hence, nothing short of a complete specification of its "aspects" or characteristics would assure us of the existence of a material object. We must rely, then, on what Price calls "perceptual assurance". Although such assurance is not " . . . *knowledge* of the material world, [it] is quite sufficient for all the purposes of Science and of daily life".[14]

In order to determine the way in which sense-data may be said to "belong to" a material object Price describes a complex process of construction (the description of which would carry us far beyond the intention of this discussion of Price's perceptual theory) which yields a unified collection of sense-data " . . . consisting of a standard solid together with a set of distortion series and a set of differentiation series" which constitute a "family of sense-data".[15] The particular data which are apprehended by a percipient in any perceptual situation are relative to the percipient's position and condition. And it is changes in these factors which yield the distortion and differentiation series. Price believes that what is suggested by the conception of families of sense-data is the notion that a family consists of " . . . an ordered system of possible sense-data".[16] The perceptible aspects of a material object consist in actual sense-data and the indefinite series of sense-data which could be perceived " . . . if an observer were at such and such a point of view . . . "[17]

The conclusions of Price's theory of perception could be said to be phenomenalistic except for the fact that Price believes that the sensible aspects of a perceptible object are not the ONLY aspects of such objects. A material thing or a "complete thing" is an entity which is "composed" of a family of sense-data with its standard solid, causative aspects and unknown characteristics. The secondary and primary qualities, though they are not "in" a thing, BELONG to the thing as parts of the family which constitute the thing. Although Price claims to be putting forward a "realistic" theory of perception, he also admits that he has incorporated many of the arguments, methods, and terms of a phenomenalistic theory of perception. Price admits that every physical object has eventually to be described in terms of sense-data. "To this extent", he writes, "the Phenomenalistic philosophers are in the right".[18]

Having examined briefly some of the essential characteristics of "traditional" phenomenalism and some of the aspects of the sense-datum theory, we will turn our attention now to a distinct, early form of phenomenalism, factual phenomenalism. Although there are basic elements of factual phenomenalism in Ernst Mach's analysis of the conception of a thing or body, the classic exponent of what R. J. Hirst has called "factual phenomenalism"[19] is Mill.

B. Factual Phenomenalism

Factual phenomenalism, according to Hirst's account, is that perceptual theory which asserts that a material thing or object consists of a group of actual and possible sense-data or sense-contents. When an object is not being perceived it consists of possible sense-data.[20]

According to Mill, we have no direct experience of material things in our perceptual experiences. We can know nothing about the external world except the sensations which we experience from it. Mill holds that all of our concepts of "physical properties" are ultimately derived from IDEAS OF SENSATION. Categorical statements about the existence of "physical objects" or "material objects" can be expressed in statements about what sensations or sense-perceptions finite perceivers may actually or possibly have under certain conditions. The uncritical, unreflective belief in the existence of physical objects actually makes no reference to anything except what we perceive or could perceive through our senses. Since, according to Mill, sensations occur in regular sequences and patterns, one sensation suggests, through a process of association, the possibility of experiencing other sensations. Such "possibilities" remain in existence even if no one is perceiving them.[21] The immediate perception of certain "ideas of sensation" suggests the possibility of experiencing other sensations if certain conditions or positions are changed. In Mill's account of perception visual sensations are considered to be "symbols of tactual and muscular ones".[22] The actual visual sensations, then, may be said to "represent" possible tactual and kinesthetic sensations. Mill illustrates what he means by possible sensations or "contingent sensations" in the following way:

> I see a piece of white paper on a table. I go into another room, and though I have ceased to see it, I am persuaded that the paper is still there. I no longer have the sensations which it gave me; but I believe that when I again place myself in the circumstances in which I had those sensations . . . when I go again into the room, I shall again have them . . . The conception I form of the world existing at any moment, comprises, along with the sensations I am feeling, a countless variety of possibilities of sensations . . . [23]

Mill defines matter as the "Permanent Possibility of Sensation" and claims that when we conceive of a material body we do so either because we have had or could have an indefinite number of sensations. The analysis of the belief that "Calcutta exists" even if it is not being perceived by myself or any other percipient or percipients, Mill asserts, means that if it were possible for a percipient individual to be in certain specific circumstances (in Mill's example, on "the banks of the Hooghly"), then he would have those sensations which would lead him to assert that Calcutta exists.[24] Material objects, for Mill, are what he describes as "fixed groups" of possible sensations. Although he does admit a nominal distinction between qualities and sensations, Mill insists that the same phenomenon when experienced along with feelings, desires and the entire "stream of consciousness" is described as a sensation; when this phenomenon occurs in what he calls a "rigid complex" it is described as a quality. Hence, Mill asserts that

> the distinction which we verbally make between the properties of things and the sensations we receive from them, must originate in the convenience of discourse rather than in the nature of what is signified by the terms.[25]

Mill seems to be saying that we may describe an object (a "rigid complex") in terms of qualities but what we immediately experience is a complex of sensations which enables us to anticipate other sensations we could experience if certain conditions were met. Actual sensations are symbols or signs of possible sensations. Those sensations which we could perceive immediately following the experience of actual sensations Mill describes as "present possibilities". Because of the constant experience of certain sensations occurring together, the presence of one "announces" the possible presence of other sensations. Mill's phenomenalistic reductionism may be described as an attempt to analyze the conception of material things in terms of the immediate or possible sensations which are (or may be) directly experienced. To say that a material thing exists would be to assert that certain sensations would occur if a particular set of conditions relating to the condition and the position of a percipient individual was fulfilled. Common objects such as trees, tables, and walls are, according to Mill's phenomenalism, analyzable into groups of actual and possible sensations. Although Mill's analysis begins as an attempt to define what is meant by a material object and is, in this sense, a linguistic analysis, the basic elements to which Mill's phenomenalism refers are not statements ABOUT actual or possible sensations, but the sensations themselves which are (or may be) experienced. Because of the factual claims implicit in Mill's phenomenalistic analysis his position must be distinguished from a later development in phenomenalistic reductionism, linguistic phenomenalism. Before turning to a brief examination of linguistic phenomenalism, it may be fruitful to recapitulate the fundamental points of Mill's analysis. Mill asserts (a) that our knowledge of the external world is derived from the sensations we experience; (b) that we cannot be said to immediately experience physical or material objects; (c) that our concepts of physical properties or qualities are derived from what Mill calls "ideas of sensation"; (d) the actual experience of certain sensations "suggests" the present possibility of experiencing other sensations; (e) sensations actually experienced (for example, visual sensations) are "symbols" of possible sensations (for example, tactual ones); (f) material objects are "fixed groups" or complexes of actual and possible sensations; (g) categorical propositions asserting the existence of some object, X, can be expressed in terms of conditional propositions which assert in the consequent what sensations would occur under such and such a set of conditions. There is a clear family resemblance between Mill's account of perception and that of Berkeley. Before discussing the nature of this resemblance it is necessary to turn our attention to the form of phenomenalism which has "superseded" factual phenomenalistic analyses like that of Mill, linguistic phenomenalism.

C. Linguistic Phenomenalism

The transition from factual to linguistic phenomenalism probably has taken place because of the general influence of linguistic analysis upon some contemporary philosophers and the subsequent tendency to conceive of analyses of perception not as THEORIES put forward to explain the facts, but as languages which state these facts with greater clarity and precision. According to linguistic phenomenalists generally, there is one set of facts (or existents) which can be described in two terminologies or languages. Thus, for example, perceptual data may be described in "material object" language or sense-data language. It is believed that the linguistic version of phenomenalism is less misleading than factual versions since it employs the hypothetical FORM of its propositions to express the possibility of perception when no perception is actually taking place. The foundation upon which linguistic reductionism builds is statements about sense-data and not, as is the case with factual phenomenalism, the immediate experience of sense-data or sensations (i.e., the experiential process of perception).

Another possible reason for the linguistic reformulation of phenomenalism would be the problem which arises out of the phenomenalistic conception of possible sense-data. According to Mill, unperceived objects may be thought of as unfulfilled possibilities of having sensations. The basic objection which has been raised against this notion is simply that when we assert that a certain unperceived object exists we intend to say that it actually exists in the same way in which objects we are actually perceiving do. That is, when we say that "X exists" we are saying not that this something, X, has only a hypothetical existence, but that it exists in the full sense of the word "existence".[26] A similar line of argument, put forward by Hirst, tries to show that it is absurd to assert that possible sense-data are constituents of material objects. Hirst argues that to affirm that an object, O, is "composed" of a sense-datum, SD, is to imply that that SD is as actual as O. Hence, to assume that O actually exists and then say that O is COMPOSED of SD implies that SD actually exists. To say, on the other hand, that SD is possible implies that SD does not or may not actually exist. The phenomenalist, then, who claims that a material object is composed of possible sense-data treats a possible sense-datum as an actual component.[27] It is clear that the same kind of objection can also be raised against linguistic forms of analysis.

Having considered some of the ostensible reasons for the transition from factual to linguistic phenomenalism, we will now examine some of the basic tenets of the linguistic version of phenomenalism. With the intention of correcting what he calls the misconception of phenomenalism, A. J. Ayer put forward the following reformulation of phenomenalism:

> the statement that material things consist of sense-data must be understood to designate . . . not a factual but a linguistic relationship. What is being claimed is simply that the propositions which are ordinarily expressed by sentences which refer to material things could also be expressed by sentences which referred exclusively to sense-data . . . possible as well as actual.[28]

It has often been noted that the actual "translation" of material object statements into sense-data statements has presented the linguistic phenomenalist with serious difficulties. This form of translation seems to encounter the problem of establishing or constructing an autonomous language of sense-data or sense-contents. If material object statements are actually translatable into sense-data statements, it seems that some paradigm translations should be provided. But, as Gilbert Ryle has said, " . . . language does not enable us to formulate the propositions into which, according to Phenomenalism, propositions about [material things] should be translatable".[29] If a material thing is conceived of as a logical construction out of sense-data, any assertion made about material things could be further reduced to statements made about sense-data or sense-contents. Such a notion encounters the additional difficulty involved in the fact that sense-data statements are inexhaustible in number and, therefore, " . . . the content of a statement about a material thing cannot be . . . specified by any finite number of references to sense-data".[30]

One of the paradoxical difficulties of linguistic phenomenalism arises out of the central part which hypothetical propositions play in this analysis of perception. It appears that in practice we have to refer to material objects in conditional statements since it seems that our language was developed to describe such objects and not sense-data. If the linguistic phenomenalist is attempting to establish a non-natural language (for example, a sense-datum language) in order to state more precisely the facts of perception, it seems odd that such a theory seems to use, unavoidably, material object expressions in a set of sense-datum statements. Although the basic formula of linguistic phenomenalism claims that any statement about a material object is equivalent to a set of statements about actual or possible sense-data, it appears that in practice material object statements are equivalent to a set of statements mentioning material objects but referring to sense-data. Although Ayer had said that "I suppose that a suitable vocabulary could be invented if some ingenious person thought it worth his trouble",[31] no such vocabulary has been constructed and this difficulty in linguistic phenomenalism is still unresolved.

In a discussion of phenomenalism Ayer stated that the phenomenalist does not deny that there are physical objects. The phenomenalist contends that if there are physical objects, they are constituted by sense-data. And his basic problem is to analyze those statements which refer to physical objects. Since it is possible that physical objects may exist unperceived, the phenomenalist will have to describe such objects, as we have seen, in terms of hypothetical assertions about what would be perceived if such and such conditions were met.[32]

The hypothetical statements used by the phenomenalist are "subjunctive conditionals" or "counterfactual conditionals" which describe not how something seems to a perceiver, but how something would seem under a specific set of conditions. To say that there is a "couch" in the living room although no one is actually perceiving it means that if, contrary to a fact, a perceiver were to enter the living room he would then perceive couch-like sense-data. Now, it is precisely against such use of subjunctive conditionals that some criticism has been leveled. Isaiah Berlin raises an objection similar to the one directed against the factual phenomenalist's conception of possible sense-data. He claims that categorical, existential material thing statements are used to

> describe something which is occurring or being characterized at the time of speaking . . . and being characterized or occurring, unless the contrary is . . . stated or implied, not intermittently but continuously, and in any case not "hypothetically." For to say that something is occurring hypothetically is a . . . artificial and misleading way of saying that it is not . . . occurring at all.[33]

Ayer defends phenomenalism against this particular attack by asserting that while it is accurate to say that statements of hypothetical form which refer to sense-data are not used to assert that any sense-data are actually occurring, this does not mean that such statements are not being used to assert that any physical events are occurring or that physical objects exist. Ayer compares the procedure of the phenomenalist to the physicist's method of replacing categorical statements about electrons by hypothetical statements about the results of physical experiments.[34] However, in an additional criticism of phenomenalism Isaiah Berlin maintains that the reduction of material object statements into sense-datum statements seems " . . . to leave something out, to substitute something intermittent and attenuated for something solid and continuous".[35] Again, Ayer defends the phenomenalistic analysis by claiming that the reductionist procedure of phenomenalism leaves nothing out of its account. For, any statement which implies that there are objects which are "solid and continuous" will appear in the form of assertions which refer to sense-data.[36] The basic phenomenalistic formula may be expressed in the following way: if it is assumed that physical objects exist, and if physical objects are said to exist even though they are not being perceived by anyone, any assertion made about the existence of physical objects can be reduced to a set of assertions about sense-data which could be, or would be, perceived under a set of given conditions. Ayer claims that, despite the difficulties which phenomenalism encounters, such a theory has received a good deal of support because the introduction of sense-data (as the immediate data apprehended in sense-experience) seemed to leave no other alternative open.[37] Basically, it appeared that if assertions made about physical objects could only be verified or falsified through the apprehension of sense-data, such statements must ultimately be reducible to assertions about sense-data. Whether Ayer's notion that phenomenalism seemed to follow in the wake of the adoption of sense-datum terminology is correct or not, it is interesting to note that H. H. Price (who, as we have seen, adopted a sense-datum terminology) regretted the fact that his theory of perception seemed to be too close to the phenomenalistic theory of perception.[38] This seems to substantiate Ayer's claim.

Although there are a number of criticisms which have been brought against the phenomenalistic theory of perception, it has not been our intention to examine such criticisms in detail – except in those instances where responses to such criticism might clarify some of the essential aspects of phenomenalism – nor has it been our intention to defend phenomenalism. Fundamentally, we have seen that we must distinguish between two basic forms of phenomenalism: factual phenomenalism (represented in this account by Ernst Mach and, primarily, by Mill) and linguistic phenomenalism (represented by Ayer's reformulation of phenomenalism). For the factual phenomenalist a material object is nothing but a complex of sensations, actual and possible. Its reductive analysis leads us back to the direct experience of sensations. This is apparent in Mill's assertion that

> Feeling and thought are much more real than anything else; they are the only things which we directly know to be real . . . All matter apart from the feelings of sentient beings has but an hypothetical and unsubstantial existence: it is a mere assumption to account for our sensations . . . [39]

The mode of phenomenalism which refers us back to immediately experienced sensations is distinct from that form of phenomenalism (adopted by Ayer under the influence of Russell and Carnap) which affirms that material objects are logical constructions out of sense-data. The factual phenomenalist does not avoid introducing mentalistic concepts which interpret our knowledge of the external world in terms of sensations or mental events "in the mind". The constructionist, on the other hand, prefers to avoid such reductionism by claiming that what we immediately perceive are sense-data, not sensations. Sense-datum terminology is adopted in many perceptual analyses, as Price has said, precisely in order to avoid any commitment to any view about the "status" of sense-data. "The term sense-datum is meant to be a *neutral term*."[40] In the case of Mill, a material object is nothing more than a "fixed group" of actual and possible sensations. For the logical constructionist, a material object is a formal construct. Mill claims that categorical assertions about the existence of material objects can be expressed in terms of hypothetical assertions about sensations. If we bear in the mind the distinction between sensations and sense-data, it may be said that Mill's analysis of material object assertions is as much a linguistic analysis as the form of the analyses adopted by A. J. Ayer. But it is obvious that Mill's reductive analysis has a factual claim, a reference to the immediate experience of sensations, which the more formal reductionism of linguistic phenomenalism tends to avoid by emphasizing that material object statements are reducible not to immediate sensation or the immediate perception of sense-data, but to STATEMENTS ABOUT what is, or could be, experienced. It is interesting to note that D. M. Armstrong, commenting on Ayer's notion that the assertion that physical objects are logical constructions out of sense-data MEANS that any physical object statement is equivalent to a set of statements about sense-data,[41] asks

> why should the Phenomenalist define his doctrine in this way? Phenomenalism is not fundamentally a doctrine of the translatability of certain sorts of statements into certain others, but is a doctrine of the nature of the physical world. For the Phenomenalist, the physical world is nothing more than sense-impressions, actual and possible.[42]

This statement by Armstrong seems to indicate that he is either unable or unwilling to accept the linguistic reformulation of phenomenalism which we have discussed above, or he has not clearly seen the intention of Ayer to transform the phenomenalistic analysis of the problems of perception. For, strictly speaking, linguistic phenomenalism cannot be considered as a doctrine about the external world or the physical world. As Warnock has remarked, the more sophisticated version of phenomenalism tried to avoid the "factual look of the claims" of phenomenalists like Mill, and substituted an analysis which was primarily a "claim about language".[43] If we draw out the implications of the linguistic phenomenalist's position, if we see, that is, that it is essentially a theory about the language of perception and not fundamentally a theory about our perception of the physical world, we can better understand the importance of the transition from factual to linguistic phenomenalism. It may be said that phenomenalism attempts to present an alternative language of perception, a language structured not, as ordinary language seems to be, in terms of material objects, but in terms of sense-data.

Although we have only briefly examined some of the aspects of the sense-datum theory and the two major forms of phenomenalism, our attention will now be focused upon the basic intention of this chapter – to attempt to indicate the precise relationship between Berkeley's theory of perception and the phenomenalistic analysis of perception.

D. Berkeley's Theory of Perception and Phenomenalism

The basic premise of phenomenalism is, as we have seen, that we do not immediately or directly perceive material objects or physical objects, but more elementary data which have been called "sensa", "sense impressions", or "sense data". Berkeley's term IDEA has often been equated with the term sense-datum. This equation, however, would seem to be too facile. Berkeley's conception of "ideas of sense" is such that it emphasizes the mentalistic or mind-dependent character of such immediate objects of sense. Since Berkeley has often spoken of ideas OR sensations, he has obviously committed himself to the view that the immediate data apprehended in sense-experience are "in the mind" or are "mental events". Now, the sense-datum terminology was adopted, as we have noted above, in order to introduce a neutral term into the analysis of perception. Ayer, in describing the immediate data of sense as "sense-contents" (which are similar to sense data), asserts that they are neither physical nor mental since "the distinction between what is mental and what is physical does not apply to sense-contents", but " . . . only to objects which are logical constructions out of them".[44] Despite the fact that G. E. Moore has maintained that the "common view" in philosophy is that sense-data exist only in our minds,[45] it has been asserted that sense-datum theorists admit that sense-data are private to the individual perceiving them without necessarily concluding "that they are mental in status or that they exist "in my mind"".[46] Although the controversy concerning the "status" of sense data is far beyond the scope of this enquiry, we must examine such a question, at least in a cursory manner, in order to establish whether, in fact, Berkeley's concept of "ideas" is similar to that of sense-data. The most succinct way of stating this relationship between sense-data and "ideas" would be the following: if sense-data are thought to exist "in the mind" or are conceived of as mental events, then they are obviously similar to Berkeley's ideas of sense; if, on the other hand, sense-data are not thought to be mind-dependent phenomena, if they are neutral data or are physical entities, then the equation between Berkeley's concept of "ideas" and sense-data cannot be made.

At any rate, it appears that there is a considerable degree of agreement between Berkeley and the phenomenalists in regard to the immediate objects of sense-perception. That is, Berkeley claims, as the phenomenalists do, that the immediate objects of sense are indubitable, momentary "entities" which exist when they are perceived. In addition, it may be said that the phenomena immediately perceived, since they are described as being related to the consciousness of a percipient individual, are not only relative existents, but are private to the individual perceiving them. According to our interpretation of Berkeley's analysis of perception, no two individual percipients can be said to perceive the same elementary data of sense. And, according to Berkeley's account of the matter, it is God who causes individual percipients to be affected by similar sense-ideas.

The identity of the objects of sense is "preserved" in the divine mind. Hence, Berkeley's "ideas of sense", like the sense-data of the phenomenalist, are private to the individual perceiving them.

A fundamental distinction which must be made between "ideas of sense" and sense-data is that the sense-datum in visual perception has been characterized as a "patch" which has a certain size, shape and color while, for Berkeley, a sense-idea is a color, a shape, a size, not a datum which HAS a certain color, shape, or size. In addition, it should be noted that at least some philosophers who have adopted the sense-datum terminology do not hesitate to assert that sense-data have the "characteristic" of depth and that "this characteristic of them is just as much "given" as colour or shape . . . "[47] Such a view is, of course, incompatible with Berkeley's basic notion that "depth" or distance is not immediately perceived, but that judgments of distance are dependent upon visual, tactual, and kinaesthetic "cues" which are the experiential data which determine such judgments. Although the distinctions we have indicated may not be of major importance, they are, nevertheless, real distinctions which should be borne in mind when an identification between Berkeley's concept of sense-ideas and that of the phenomenalist's sense-data is put forward too dogmatically.

If we grant that there is at least a similarity between sense-ideas and sense-data even though there are basic distinctions between the two ways of describing such data, then we may proceed to see what relationship can be established between Berkeley's perceptual analysis and the two major forms of phenomenalism we have briefly examined.

Before passing on to a consideration of the comparison between Berkeley's perceptual analysis and what we have described as factual phenomenalism, it may be fruitful to see what relationship, if any, the Russellian construction of the external world (in his early philosophical work) has with some of Berkeley's methods of analysis.

If we overlook, for the moment, the distinctions which we have already pointed out between ideas of sense and sense-data, and if the interpretation of Berkeley's theory – put forward in Chapter III – is valid, we may say that there is a certain resemblance between Russell's notion that a "thing" may be identified with the class of its appearances and Berkeley's notion that a thing is a collection of actual and possible sense-ideas. It had been argued that, for Berkeley, a thing cannot be considered as a datum. Since he had said that we immediately perceive sense-ideas in sense-experience and that things are congeries of ideas – apparent size, apparent shape, apparent color, etc., – it might be possible to assert that, for Berkeley, a THING is also a system of appearances.[48] If the word system is being used in its conventional sense, if, that is, it means a set or arrangement of elements so related or connected as to form a unity, then such a term would not be foreign to the Berkeleyan conception of a "thing" as it has been interpreted in this enquiry. The colligation of sense-ideas, it has been argued, is a synthetic act of unification, an act by which the data apprehended by the various modalities of sense are "joined together" to form what we have described as a phenomenal object (or thing). Both Berkeley and the early Russell seem to share a certain methodological tendency. Both seem intent upon preserving the multiplicity of appearances apprehended in sense-perception without introducing occult entities (substances or substrata) which underlie these appearances. Both employ a reductive method: things for Berkeley are reduced to collections of ideas; for Russell things are reduced to "systems of appearances" or "momentary sets of sense-data". However, when Russell introduces a complex process of logical constructionism into his construction of the external world, his method has passed far beyond Berkeley's method of analysis. There is only a vague, inchoate suggestion in Berkeley's analysis of anything resembling "constructionism". Berkeley has written that

> A cherry . . . is nothing but a congeries of sensible impressions, or ideas perceived by various senses; which ideas are united into one thing . . . by the mind.[49]

Berkeley does not delve into the means by which "ideas are united into one thing" nor does he explicitly state by what mental act such unification is carried out. Basically, Russell's constructionism involves the substitution of a symbol whose denotation is given in sense-experience for a symbol whose denotation is not given in sense-experience, but is an inferred entity. Berkeley, of course, never explicitly asserts that a sensible thing is a symbol for anything. It may be said, however, that Berkeley occasionally describes an object in such a way as to suggest that the word used to identify a certain congeries of "ideas" could be said to symbolize that collection of sense-ideas. Thus, for example, he affirms that the word "apple" signifies or stands for a certain color, taste, smell, figure, and "consistence" which have been experienced as appearing together in the past.[50] Again, when he asserts that the word "die" does not denote a "substance" which is distinct from the "ideas" out of which the die is composed, we could interpret this to mean that the word "die" is simply a symbol for certain specific sensory data.[51]

Whether this somewhat tenuous relationship between certain aspects of Russell's early thought and Berkeley's analyses has any significant value or not, it may enable us to clarify more precisely Berkeley's basic position. Before we proceed to show the relationship between Mill's phenomenalism and Berkeley's perceptual analysis, we will consider one final aspect of Russell's constructive analysis. That is, his conception of "sensibilia".

Russell had said that we have no means of ascertaining how things appear from places in which there are no percipient individuals. He asserts, however, that "continuity makes it not unreasonable to suppose that they present SOME appearance at such places. Any such appearance would be included among *sensibilia*."[52] *Sensibilia*, as we have said, have the same physical and metaphysical status as sense-data except that they are data for no one. Sensibilia are said to become sense-data by entering into the relationship of acquaintance. What is given in immediate sense-experience, according to Russell, is never a thing, but only one or more of the "sensibilia" which compose the thing.[53] Russell's conception of sensibilia is put forward in order to account for the continuity of experience and possible perception. Thus, it is asserted that

> Besides the appearances which a given thing in the room presents to the actual [perceivers] . . . there are, we may suppose, other appearances which it would present to other possible [perceivers].[54]

Although it has been maintained that Russell's account of unperceived "entities" in terms of sensibilia avoids the kind of criticism which is brought against the phenomenalist's conception of possible sense-data[55] (that is, that unperceived entities are not MERE possibilities but actual existents), it appears that Russell's conception might be said to encounter a similar difficulty. For, Russell says, quite clearly, that sensibilia are, like the phenomenalist's possible sensations or possible sense-data, "hypothetical" entities.[56] Indeed, the supposition of sensibilia is to be interpreted as an "illustrative hypothesis".[57] Although Russell had described a thing as a logical construction out of sense-data and although he had asserted that "whenever possible, logical constructions are to be substituted for inferred entities",[58] he admits that sensibilia are "inferred entities".[59] In effect, it appears that Russell has said that things are logical constructions out of sense-data (which he claims are sensibilia); hence, a logical construction, which is supposed to be substituted for inferred entities, is composed out of sensibilia which are inferred entities. Whether this seemingly paradoxical formulation of Russell's analysis could or could not be resolved is a question which is, of course, beyond the scope of this investigation. This digression has, at any rate, served to indicate further distinctions which should be made between Berkeley's perceptual analysis and some of the aspects of other enquiries which seem to be superficially related to that analysis. Thus, for example, although the early writings of Russell tend to agree with Berkeley's view that the immediate data of sense-experience are not things, but more "primitive" data, it must be borne in mind that sense-data, for Russell, are "physical" and Berkeley's "ideas of sense" are, of course, "mental" or mind-dependent. Again, though some authors have referred to Berkeley's conception of possible perceptions as similar to the conception of sensibilia,[60] the distinction between the two notions should be made clear. Sensibilia are described by Russell, at one point in his discussion, as particular existents which are not dependent upon an actual percipient for their existence. Russell does not hesitate to assert that sensibilia are appearances which are independent of percipient individuals and that these appearances are "presented" by things.[61] Berkeley, of course, would maintain that there can be no appearances which exist apart from perceivers. The "permanence" of unperceived existents, in Berkeley's theory of perception, is guaranteed by the existence of a supra-phenomenal being who acts as spiritual cause of sense-ideas. The unperceived entities are not, however, PERCEIVED by God. For, he has explicitly stated that

> God . . . perceives nothing by sense as we do . . . such a Being as this can suffer nothing, nor be affected with any . . . sensation at all.[62]

Perception, as we have seen elsewhere, is a passive, receptive process for Berkeley. Since God is a purely active being, He cannot be said to PERCEIVE anything. "There is no sense nor sensory, nor any thing like a sense or sensory, in God."[63] Objects unperceived by finite individuals may be said to subsist in the divine mind. That is,

> All objects are eternally known by God, or, which is the same thing, have an eternal existence in His mind.[64]

The apparent difficulties which such a view seems to encounter are discussed above in the section on "phenomenal appearances". We can see, at any rate, that Berkeley's concept of possible perceptions cannot, strictly speaking, be identified with Russell's concept of sensibilia.

Berkeley, as we shall see, has two ways of accounting for, or referring to, perceptible phenomena. On the one hand, unperceived entities are said to continue to exist as objects of the divine mind. On the other hand, unperceived entities may be accounted for as possible sense-ideas which would be perceived under certain conditions. The second way in which Berkeley accounts for entities not actually perceived is one which will be considered in the following attempt to establish the relationship between Berkeley's perceptual theory and the two major forms of phenomenalism we have examined above.

E. Berkeley and Factual Phenomenalism

The first and foremost distinction which must be made between Berkeley's perceptual analysis and the phenomenalism of Mill is simply that, for Berkeley, matter or material substance does not exist, while for Mill, material objects are said to exist. Of course, Mill has, as it were, re-defined what it means to assert that matter exists. But Berkeley would not have been willing to meet Mill halfway and grant to matter a "hypothetical" existence. Berkeley tends to think that if matter or material substance is adequate for an explanation of the system of appearances we perceive, then either God is an unnecessary hypothesis or God is identical with matter.[65] Although Berkeley would deny that there are material objects, he does not, to be sure, deny that there are bodies or sensible objects.[66] That is, phenomenal objects or things as constructs.

Despite the fact that Mill does not hesitate to speak about MATERIAL objects and Berkeley insists that no such objects exist, Mill's account of present possibilities of sensation is reminiscent of, and derived from, Berkeley's analysis of perception. Berkeley's formula, *esse est percipi*, does tend to account for the relative existence of what is apprehended in actual perception. But, as A. A. Luce has recently said,

> Berkeley realized that the things we see and touch must continue to exist over the gaps in actual perception. In a tenable immaterialism possible perception must have its proper place, side by side with actual perception; and once committed to the Principle, *esse est percipi*, he was bound to follow it up with *esse est posse percipi*.[67]

Although Mill seems to say that the "possibilities" he refers to exist even when they are not perceived by anyone and that their existence is not dependent upon a divine mind, Berkeley maintains that possible perceptions do not exist independent of ALL minds, but may be said to be actual existents insofar as they are objects of an eternal mind. It is interesting to note that Mill's conception of possible sensations seems to encounter the difficulty which is often raised against non-linguistic forms of phenomenalism – the problem, examined above, of asserting the actual existence of possibilities – while Berkeley's position seems to avoid such a criticism by saying that what are possible perceptions for finite minds are actual existents "in" the divine mind.[68] Mill's position seems to involve him in a related difficulty which seems alien to Berkeley's analysis. For, the permanence of the "possibilities of sensation" seems to be dependent upon what Mill has described as the hypothetical existence of matter. For Berkeley, there is no need to introduce a hypothetical existent to "account for sensations" since God is the actually existing cause of sense-ideas. The order and permanence of the system of appearances which is or may be perceived by finite individuals is guaranteed by the existence of God.

In regard to the sequence and pattern of the occurrence of sensations, Mill, following Berkeley (and, of course, Hume), adopts a "regularity theory" which enables him to account for ostensible causal relations between sensations wholly in terms of sequences or correlations of phenomena. According to Mill's phenomenalistic analysis of the relation between sensations,

> It is held . . . that the . . . relation between phenomena is that of succession, and . . . that the necessity of this relation does not lie in the terms of the relation, but in a law, a uniformity, or a rule under which the terms are subsumed.[69]

The order and regularity of "ideas of sense", in Berkeley's theory, is maintained by God as spiritual cause of ideas. The relation between sense-ideas is explained by Berkeley in terms of signs. That is, ideas actually perceived or immediately perceived serve as signs of what may be perceived. Berkeley's analysis of the relationship between ideas leads him to his conception of mediate perception which is the means by which what Mill called "present possibilities" are incorporated into his theory of perception.

The concept of mediate perception is undoubtedly one of the basic phenomenalistic notions in Berkeley's analysis of perception. Employing his associationist terminology, Berkeley maintains that ideas which are "observed to go together" are "joined together" to form an object or thing. What may be called the "complete" object or thing is not immediately perceived. Hence, an object is not simply a collection of ideas actually perceived, but an entity composed of actually perceived sense-ideas and possible ideas which may, under certain conditions, be perceived. Berkeley expresses this in the following way:

> We may, from the experience we have had of the train and succession of ideas in our minds, often make . . . sure and well-grounded predictions concerning the ideas we shall be affected with pursuant to a . . . train of actions, and be enabled to pass a right judgment of what would have appeared to us, in case we were placed in circumstances very different from those we are in at present.[70]

What is immediately perceived "suggests to the mind" what might be perceived under certain conditions. When Mill claims that visual sensations are "symbols" of tactual and kinaesthetic sensations, he has explicitly adopted the Berkeleyan conception of signification. Mill's account of possible sensations – which is an essential part of his phenomenalism – is clearly indebted to Berkeley. For, he had insisted that common objects – tables, chairs, desks – could be analyzed into groups or collections of ideas. But while Berkeley claims that objects are collections of qualities or of sensations, Mill asserts that all objects are collections of SENSATIONS, actual and possible. Aside from this rather slight distinction, it could be said that Mill has followed Berkeley almost verbatim in his description of objects as complexes of sensations and his adoption of the "doctrine of suggestion".

Berkeley and Mill also share, in their basic analyses, a tendency to describe possible perceptions in factual terms. Berkeley, for example, has said that although we do not perceive any motion of the earth, we would be in error if we assumed that if we were situated at a great distance from the earth we would not then perceive the motion of the planet.[71] Mill's account of contingent sensations also contains obvious factual references. For, Mill claims that there is an "outward world" which we know by means of our actual and possible sensations. Both Berkeley and Mill, in their most typical formulations of the conception of sensible objects in the one instance and material objects in the other, seem to employ what Rudolf Carnap described as a "material mode of speech". Paul Marhenke, commenting on the distinction between material modes of speech and formal modes of speech, claims that the phenomenalistic analysis which uses material modes of speech APPEARS to provide information about the external world or physical objects. Marhenke notes that

> earlier phenomenalists showed a preference for the material mode of speech . . . Phenomenalism is . . . defined . . . when the material mode is employed . . . as the philosophical theory which holds that physical objects are . . . constructions out of sense-data [or] (1) physical objects are permanent possibilities of sensations, (2) physical objects are complexes of actual and possible sensations, (3) physical objects are classes . . . of sense-data.[72]

There is little doubt that Berkeley and Mill appear to employ material modes of speech. However, it is somewhat misleading to say that Berkeley, for example, preferred the material mode of speech since, obviously, he did not possess this conceptual-linguistic form nor does he consistently formulate his central dicta as purely linguistic forms of expression or as proposals to use concepts in a specific way. To be sure, there are occasions when he is presenting linguistic and conceptual proposals without claiming any factual reference or without inscribing pseudo-object statements. But he is not consistent in this regard and often uses expressions which "look like" the material mode of speech and yet, in his elaborations on such statements, he indicates that he is not talking in terms of meta-linguistic descriptions, but he is putting forward putative factual statements. There are instances, of course, in which Berkeley does adopt a linguistic approach in his analysis of perception.[73] Thus, for example, he says that

> The table I write on I say exists — that is, I see and feel it; and if I were out of my study I should say it existed — meaning thereby that if I was in my study I might perceive it.[74]

This analysis of Berkeley's could be translated into the material or formal modes of speech familiar in contemporary linguistic phenomenalist's methods of analysis. To assert the "existence" of a "table" or an "object" which is not being perceived MEANS that if a perceiver were in such and such a position, then he would perceive that collection of sense-contents we have learned to identify as a "table". It is clear, however, that when Berkeley (if we allow the anachronism) uses, or seems to use, a material mode of speech, this is purely accidental. In one sense, he appears to be formulating a phenomenalistic language, but, in another sense, he clearly intends to make an ontic or factual reference. This is not due to a misinterpretation of the material mode of speech, but it is due to the fact that he was unable to anticipate Carnap's formalism even though he occasionally does endeavor to adopt his own artificial language (e.g., the collection theory of objects). It will be noticed that in Berkeley's analysis of what we may call "sensible object statements" and in Mill's similar analysis, there is a reference to possible perceptions which could be immediately experienced. For Berkeley, the assertion "X exists" (though it is unperceived)

MEANS that, if a perceiver were to undertake such and such actions, then he would PERCEIVE this object. Mill also avers that to say that "X exists" though it is not being perceived means that if a percipient individual were to be in certain specific circumstances, then he would EXPERIENCE or HAVE certain sensations. Although Berkeley and Mill seem to employ ostensible material modes of speech in some of their analyses of assertions made about unperceived sensible or material objects, their analyses involve a reduction to immediate perception or immediate sensations, not to STATEMENTS ABOUT what is immediately experienced or perceived. Hence, their statements would be characterized by Carnap as pseudo-object statements.

Although it has been said that the phenomenalistic analysis in Berkeley's theory of perception "is not a suggestion that he develops",[75] this appears to be an inaccurate statement. For, the analysis of categorical existential statements about sensible objects in terms of reduction to actual and possible perceptions is implicitly present in much of Berkeley's analysis of perception. If our interpretation of Berkeley's perceptual analysis is reasonably accurate, then it must be said that, according to Berkeley, sensible objects are not immediately perceived and are congeries of sense-ideas. Now, if an object is a collection of sense-ideas, and if this object is, as it were, "constructed" out of actual and possible sense-ideas, then it is apparent that statements made about the existence of such objects could be reduced to immediately or mediately perceived sense-contents. Translating Berkeley into the language of factual phenomenalism, we may that the assertion "There is a table in my study" (even though no one is perceiving that congeries of sense-data we identify as a "table") means that if I were to enter my study, then I would perceive "table-like" sense-data or I would perceive a specific congeries of sense-data which I have come to signify by the name "table". Berkeley's phenomenalistic analysis is manifest in his conception of possible sense-data and mediate perception. He has said that

> we may . . . be said to perceive sensible things mediately by sense . . . when, from a frequently perceived connexion, the immediate perception of ideas by

> one sense *suggests* . . . others . . . belonging to another sense, which are wont to be connected with them.[76]

Thus, when we say that we "hear" an automobile even though we have only perceived certain specific sounds, we mean that if we were to enter into a certain set of conditions, then we would perceive "automobile-like" sense-data which we have come to associate with certain aural sense-data. Mediate perception is the process by which we anticipate sense-experiences through the imaginative representation of possible data which we have come to associate with specific immediately perceived ideas.[77] There seems to be an intimate relationship between Berkeley's conceptions of mediate perception, possible sense-ideas, and his phenomenalistic analysis of categorical existential statements. It may be said, then, that Berkeley's perceptual analysis is closely related to that form of phenomenalism which is derived from that analysis, factual phenomenalism, and is clearly distinct from the formalistic appeal to meaning postulates or prescriptive linguistic forms.

F. Berkeley and Linguistic Phenomenalism

Although passing references to the relationship between Berkeley's theory of perception and linguistic phenomenalism have already been made, we will attempt to indicate more specifically what this relationship — if it truly exists — is. We have already seen that Berkeley's phenomenalism appears to include a factual content which linguistic phenomenalism intended to expunge. Ayer, for example, insists upon the adoption of what Carnap had called "formal modes of speech". The linguistic version of phenomenalism seems to "lead us back" not to immediate experience itself, not to Berkeley's sense-ideas or Mill's sensations, but to a set of sense-data STATEMENTS about what is experienced. This more "sophisticated" form of phenomenalism attempts to avoid material modes of speech because of the tendency to interpret "pseudo-object sentences" as statements which have reference to the structure or composition of physical objects. Rudolf Carnap had averred that pseudo-object statements

> are formulated as though they refer to . . . objects, while in reality they refer to syntactical forms, and specifically, to the forms of the designation of those objects with which they appear to deal.[78]

It is believed that formal modes of speech enable us to assert genuine object statements. When the formal mode of speech is used, this form of phenomenalism may be defined as

> the philosophical theory which holds that statements about physical objects are reducible to statements about sense-data . . . variants of this definition are obtained by substituting for the phrase "statements about physical objects are reducible . . . " one of the following phrases: (1) statements about physical objects are analyzable into statements about sense-data, (2) statements about physical objects are translatable into statements about sense-data, (3) statements about physical objects are synonymous with statements about sense-data.[79]

The obvious formal character of such various definitions of linguistic phenomenalism serves to distinguish this type of phenomenalism from the "factual" reductionism of Berkeley and Mill. The distinction between Berkeley's phenomenalistic analyses and linguistic phenomenalism is not only one of method, but of intention as well.

Despite his obvious concern with language, Berkeley did not intend to analyze the way in which we "speak about" the phenomena apprehended in perception. His introduction of a trans-phenomenal cause of the appearances which are apprehended by finite minds in sense-experience indicates his concern with a metaphysical conception and not merely with a linguistic analysis of the language of perception. Indeed, for Berkeley, phenomenalism entails theism. It is for this reason that some caution must be observed when Berkeley is made to champion the view that an analysis of language is the only proper and fruitful method in philosophy. The method of linguistic analysis, the method of linguistic phenomenalism, takes on such sophistication and formalism that it appears to be completely incompatible with the spirit and intention of Berkeley's theory of perception. To be sure, there are in Berkeley's writings inchoate attempts to adopt linguistic methods of analysis. But it must be maintained that Berkeley's primary emphasis is on being and existence, not on the way in which we "talk about" being and the existent. In addition, Berkeley seems to be essentially concerned with the ontological "status" of the *percipi* and not with the purely formal structure of assertions about what is perceived. The metaphysical aspects of Berkeley's attempt to "explain the phenomena" seem to estrange him from the contemporary phenomenalism which is primarily concerned with an analysis of the language of perception. Berkeley's phenomenalism seems to be a form of experiential or factual phenomenalism, not linguistic phenomenalism. Although Berkeley was concerned, as we have said, with language and its proper use, he also intended to put forward an interpretation of the nature of reality, an interpretation which obviously transcends the limits of a formal analysis of perceptual language. Berkeley was interested not only in attempting to deliver himself from "the deception of words", but in attempting to establish the nature of the concrete existent and the being of that transcendental reality he described as God.

Perhaps the one instance of Berkeley's adoption of a purely linguistic analysis, apart from the rudimentary forms of such analyses we have already considered, is to be found in his analysis of the proposition, "A die is hard, extended, and square." Berkeley affirms that

> to me a die seems to be nothing distinct from those things which are termed its . . . accidents. And, to say a die is hard, extended, and square is not to attribute those qualities to a subject distinct from and supporting them, but only an explication of the meaning of the word "die."[80]

If we extend this mode of analysis to relate it to the mode of speech used by the linguistic phenomenalists, we could say that statements made about the existence of "dies" could be translated into statements made about sense-contents. But this form of language analysis is not a method pursued by Berkeley to any great extent. For, Berkeley was not only interested in analyzing what it means to say that something exists or in explicating the meaning of words used to "signify" common objects. In order to "identify" a specific congeries of sense-ideas as a "die", we must first have experienced these sense-ideas in perception.[81] The phenomena signified by the word "die" are "given", and are immediate data of sense which are "imprinted" on our senses; they are "real", if relative, existents. Our object-language, Berkeley insists, has reference not merely to statements about more immediate data, sense-ideas, but to perceptual experience in its concrete immediacy. Berkeley's reductive analysis, as we have attempted to show, is concerned with a phenomenal description of the immediate experience of sensory data. It is not clear that Berkeley intended to adopt the method of analysis illustrated in the quotation referred to above. For, one problem which such a method would immediately encounter is simply that it would be impossible to provide a complete explication of the meaning of the word "die", since any object, as a collection of sense-ideas, must be a collection of an inexhaustible number of sense-ideas. Thus, as G. J. Warnock has said,

> when I say what object it is that I perceive, I am referring to a collection of ideas not all of which I am at the time perceiving – most of them are merely *suggested* by the ideas that I actually perceive . . . strictly, . . . I ought not to say that I perceive the object, but only those ideas from the object-constituting collection which I now actually perceive.[82]

Having committed himself to the view that we immediately perceive apparent color, apparent size, apparent shape, etc.,[83] Berkeley must maintain that any sensible object is "composed" of a multiplicity of sense-ideas. And, if this is the case, it is obvious that no individual percipient could perceive what may be called the "total" object; hence, a phenomenal object must be a "construct" which is formed out of the "selective" colligation of specific sensory data. Hence, the statement "A die is hard, extended, and square" is not, strictly speaking, an explication of the word "die" at all. For, if the word "die" signifies a congeries of sense-data, it surely does not signify only the data of hardness, extension, and squareness. Although it is not being argued that Berkeley was aware of the implications of his position in this regard, it appears that his factual or experiential analysis of the problems of perception is more consistent with his general theory of perception. Hence, it is not accurate to say he employed "material modes of speech".

Perhaps it may be said that Berkeley announced linguistic intentions by claiming that he would speak with the vulgar and think with the learned. Berkeley's notebook reflects this intention in a number of references. He claims that "I side in all things with the Mob."[84] He reminds himself that "we must with the Mob place certainty in the senses".[85] In regard to such assertions, A. A. Luce has maintained that this emphasis marks "Berkeley's intellectual return to the common sense of the common man after his involvement with continental skepticism and . . . Malebranche".[86] In his *Dialogues between Hylas and Philonous* Berkeley makes a commitment similar to the one he makes in the notebook. He proclaims himself a defender of "Common Sense" against the "absurdities" of skepticism and materialism.

The most obvious question we may ask in regard to this ostensible linguistic proposal is, in what sense can Berkeley be said to have spoken with the "vulgar"? Does the common man say that "things are collections of ideas" or "sensations concreted together"? Does the non-philosopher believe that God is the cause of our sensations? Is Berkeley speaking with the common man when he says that we perceive apparent color, apparent size, apparent figure, etc.? Is it a common sense notion that God is the guarantor of the "permanence" and identity of objects? Does the ordinary man believe or say that statements about the existence of sensible things can be expressed in terms of statements which refer to possible perceptions? Does the common man, for that matter, say or believe that we perceive "ideas"? Does he affirm that the things we perceive are "in the mind"? Would the ordinary man ever say that the things perceived by finite minds have only a "relative existence"? Would any common man ever assert that there are ideas which have an "ectypal" existence in finite minds and others which have an "archetypal" existence in the divine mind? It appears that, as a matter of fact, Berkeley did not follow through with his ostensible intention to "speak with the vulgar".

Although he does not deny the existence of bodies or sensible things – and in this regard he does reflect common-sense beliefs – , it is difficult to believe that the means by which he "preserved" the existence of common sense objects is compatible either with the beliefs of the common man or with ordinary language. Of course, it has been argued throughout that Berkeley's concept of perception is not a form of common sense realism or naive realism, but a species of phenomenalism. At any rate, it is believed that Berkeley did not remain consistent with his ostensible intention to "speak with the vulgar". Again, it is not being denied that Berkeley was, as a matter of fact, concerned with linguistic problems, with the use and abuse of language. But it has been argued that he essentially uses ontic modes of speech and that his theory is not fundamentally a formal examination of the language of perception, but a description of the process of perceptual experience.

It appears that there are only occasional and rudimentary instances in which Berkeley seems to adopt a linguistic mode of analysis. His account of perception cannot be said to be related to linguistic phenomenalism for a number of reasons. (1) The linguistic phenomenalist claims that what we immediately perceive are sense-data, not sensations or "ideas". But Berkeley's analysis of perception is based upon the immediate perception of sense-ideas which are relative, particular, mind-dependent existents. Sense-data (as described by the linguistic phenomenalist) are neither mental nor physical entities. Hence, we cannot equate the concept of the immediate data of the linguistic phenomenalist with Berkeley's "ideas". (2) While the phenomenalists who have adopted a method of linguistic analysis declare that they do not intend to provide information about the composition of physical objects,[87] Berkeley does not hesitate to assert that "bodies" or "sensible objects" ARE nothing more than collections of sense-ideas, actual and possible. (3) The reductionism of the most recent form of phenomenalism leads to assertions ABOUT actual or possible sense-data. With some exceptions, Berkeley's method of analysis is a form of reductionism which is the result of a phenomenology of concrete, immediate sense-experience. (4) Berkeley's method of analysis could be interpreted in terms of the use of ostensible material modes of speech while the linguistic phenomenalists insist upon using only formal modes of speech because they are less misleading that the former.[88] (5) The linguistic phenomenalists do not deny the existence of material objects and, in fact, claim that "the determination of the composition of material objects [is] the prerogative of the scientist . . . "[89] Berkeley, of course, has directed his polemics against the existence of such entities. To be sure, he does say that one may

> retain the word Matter, and apply it to the objects of sense, if you please; provided you do not attribute to them any subsistence distinct from their being perceived.[90]

(6) The contemporary phenomenalist's method of analysis involves the notion that when we talk about unperceived objects we are talking about the possibility of experiencing certain sense-data. D. M. Armstrong has said that this does not mean

> that we are talking about the mere possibility of the existence of physical objects. We are talking about the *actual*, not the hypothetical, existence of certain unobserved physical objects.[91]

The phenomenalists, according to Armstrong and others, seem to be saying that we may talk about mere possibilities or hypothetical existents even though we are ostensibly referring to actually existing physical objects. Berkeley's conception of possible perceptions appears to resemble this kind of formulation even though he would not assert that a finite consciousness could KNOW about the ACTUAL EXISTENCE of physical objects. What is not perceived by a finite percipient is "known" by God. (7) Linguistic phenomenalists have, under the influence of the early writings of Bertrand Russell and the early work of Rudolf Carnap,[92] claimed that physical objects are logical constructions out of sense-data. Ayer has presented a clear explication of the method of logical construction. He asserts that

> to say that a symbol is constituted by signs which are identical with one another in their sensible form . . . is not to say that a symbol is a collection . . .

> of sense-contents. For when we speak of certain objects, *b, c, d* . . . as being elements of an object *e*, and of *e* as being constituted by *b, c, d* . . . we are not saying that they form a part of *e*, in the sense in which my arm is a part of my body . . . What we are saying is that all the sentences in which the symbol *e* occurs can be translated into sentences which do not contain *e* itself . . . but do contain symbols *b, c, d* . . . In such a case we say that *e* is a logical construction out of *b, c, d*.[93]

Now, although it has been argued that Berkeley's analysis of perception includes an implicit, if inchoate, constructionism, it certainly contains nothing like the method of logical constructionism which Ayer has described. In fact, it is probable that Ayer introduces such a method of analysis in order to overcome or avoid the FACTUAL or empirical reference which Berkeley's conception of objects as congeries of sense-contents seems to imply. Indeed, Ayer remarks that the assertion that objects (for example, tables) are logical constructions out of sense-data "is not a factual assertion at all".[94] The constructionism which, as we have argued, is present in rudimentary form in Berkeley's writings[95] is expressed in rather vague statements which claim that sensible things are groups of sense-data "concreted together" or are collections of sense-data "joined together" by an intentional mental act. Berkeley avers that

> men combine together several ideas, apprehended by divers senses . . . observed to have some connexion . . . either with respect to co-existence or succession; all which they refer to one name, and consider as one thing.[96]

Despite the vagueness of Berkeley's statements about the way in which we "combine together" the various sensory data apprehended by the modalities of sense, it has been argued that Berkeley intended, or should have intended, to assert that the diverse data which are perceived are synthesized into the unity of a thing or object. It has been argued that this act of synthesis does not take place in perception itself since Berkeley has clearly described perception as a passive, receptive process, but is an act of imagination.[97] And, since Berkeley has attributed the "image-forming-power" (Cp. the German *Einbildungskraft*) to will, the synthetic act of "joining together" the various sense-ideas is an act of volition. The point of this discussion, however, is simply to indicate that

Berkeley's constructionism cannot be identified with Ayer's notion that physical objects are constructions out of sense-data. Hence, a too facile identification of contemporary phenomenalism with Berkeley's perceptual analysis cannot be supported.

It may be concluded that Berkeley's species of phenomenalism is clearly related to that mode of phenomenalism – Mill's factual phenomenalism – which is itself derived from Berkeley's theory of perception. But, as we have seen, the relation between Berkeley's phenomenalistic position and that of Mill is not one of identity, but of resemblance. The contemporary forms of phenomenalism, however, are only tangentially related to Berkeley's analysis of perception. The essential core of Berkeley's thought is metaphysical, an interpretation of the nature of reality which attempts to transcend a purely phenomenalistic reductionism. The phenomenalism is, to be sure, there; but it entails theism. For, Berkeley does not restrict knowledge to phenomena alone nor does he say that the ultimate existents are sense-ideas or phenomenal objects. He does, however, restrict knowledge derived from sense-perception to phenomena, to the multiplicity of sense-phenomena perceived and to the phenomenal objects which are "constructions" out of such data. Berkeley contends that sense-experience is an apprehension of impermanent, fleeting, perishable phenomena. Perhaps the only inaccessible elements in Berkeley's theory of knowledge, if such they may be called, are the ideas in the divine mind. Since "all objects are eternally known by God, or . . . have an eternal existence in His mind,"[98] and since God knows and comprehends the REAL objects,[99] we must conclude that what man apprehends in perception and the objects which are derived from perceptual data are not ultimately real. Berkeley has precluded the possibility that we may be said to know what is in the divine mind by his desire to avoid Malebranche's notion that we have access to the context of a divine consciousness. At any rate, it appears that the phenomenalistic aspects of Berkeley's thought are subordinate to his total metaphysical conception. To hail Berkeley as a precursor of linguistic phenomenalism or of (say) Austin's linguistic phenomenology is not faithful to the metaphysical content of Berkeley's analysis of perception. One may feel that metaphysical appeals distort the clarity of his thought, but one distorts Berkeley's philosophical intentions if they are ignored. Despite his concern with language, he was not a linguistic reductionist; for, he is concerned not only with how we talk about the world or experience, but with the ontological status of human experience, the phenomena encountered in perception, with a description of HOW man experiences a multiplicity of diverse cognitive and sensory phenomena. He was not only concerned with how we use the word "existence", but with the complexity of existence itself. Berkeley's phenomenalism is an attempt to describe or explain (he does both) the facts of perception. Sometimes he seems to anticipate a method of constructionism (as J. O. Urmson points out in his *Philosophical Analysis*) and sometimes he seems to anticipate linguistic phenomenalism; but it can also be said that Berkeley comes close to providing a rudimentary phenomenology of perception which is not wholly unlike that of contemporary phenomenologists.

Notes

1 Wilfrid Sellars, *Science, Perception and Reality* (New York, 1963), p. 60.

2 H. H. Price, *Perception* (London, 1932), p. 3.

3 Gilbert Ryle, *The Concept of Mind* (London, 1949), p. 216.

4 G. E. Moore, *Some Main Problems of Philosophy* (New York, 1962), p. 48.

5 Bertrand Russell, *Mysticism and Logic* (New York, 1957), p. 148.

6 Ernst Mach, *The Analysis of Sensations* (New York, 1959), pp. 6-7.

7 Bertrand Russell, *Our Knowledge of the External World* (New York, 1960), pp. 72-74.

8 Bertrand Russell, *The Problems of Philosophy* (London, 1912), pp. 178-179.

9 Rudolf Carnap, *Der Logische Aufbau der Welt* (Berlin, 1928), p. 91.

10 A. J. Ayer, *Language, Truth and Logic* (New York, n.d.), p. 123.

11 B. Russell, *Mysticism and Logic*, p. 150.

12 H. H. Price, *op. cit.*, p. 145f.

13 *Ibid.*

14 *Ibid.*, p. 203.

15 *Ibid.*, p. 227.

16 *Ibid.*, p. 264.

17 *Ibid.*, p. 284.

18 *Ibid.*, p. 298.

19 R. J. Hirst, *The Problems of Perception* (London, 1959), p. 76.

20 *Ibid.*, p. 80.

21 John S. Mill, *An Examination of Sir William Hamilton's Philosophy* (London, 1865), p. 196.

22 *Ibid.*, p. 237.

23 J. V. Canfield and F. H. Donnell, eds., *Readings in the Theory of Knowledge* (New York, 1964), p. 457.

24 John S. Mill, *op. cit.*, p. 246.

25 John S. Mill, *A System of Logic* (London, 1843), I, iii, 9.

26 D. M. Armstrong, *Perception and the Physical World*, p. 54.

27 R. J. Hirst, *op. cit.*, p. 81.

28 A. J. Ayer, *The Foundations of Empirical Knowledge* (London, 1958), p. 232.

29 Gilbert Ryle, *op. cit.*, pp. 234-235.

30 A. J. Ayer, *op. cit.*, p. 240.

31 A. J. Ayer, *Philosophical Essays* (London, 1954), p. 134.

32 A. J. Ayer, *The Problem of Knowledge* (London, 1956), pp. 119-120.

33 Isaiah Berlin, "Empirical Propositions and Hypothetical Statements", *Mind*, LIX, 300-301.

34 A. J. Ayer, *The Problem of Knowledge*, p. 121.

35 Isaiah Berlin, *op. cit.*, p. 291.

36 A. J. Ayer, *op. cit.*, p. 122.

37 *Ibid.*, p. 129.

38 H. H. Price, *Perception*, p. vii.

39 J. S. Mill, *Three Essays on Religion* (London, 1874), p. 198.

40 H. H. Price, *op. cit.*, p. 19.

41 A. J. Ayer, *Philosophical Essays*, p. 125.

42 D. M. Armstrong, *op. cit.*, p. 48.

43 G. J. Warnock, *Berkeley*, p. 237.

44 A. J. Ayer, *Language, Truth and Logic*, p. 123.

45 George E. Moore, *Some Main Problems of Philosophy*, p. 57.

46 Gilbert Ryle, *op. cit.*, p. 211.

47 H. H. Price, *op. cit.*, p. 218.

48 Berkeley, *D.H.P.*, III, pp. 315, 336.

49 *Ibid.*, p. 324.

50 Berkeley, *Principles* . . . , Section 1.

51 *Ibid.*, Section 59.

52 Bertrand Russell, *Mysticism and Logic*, pp. 144-145.

53 *Ibid.*, p. 168.

54 *Ibid.*, p. 149.

55 D. M. Armstrong *op. cit.*, p. 54n.

56 B. Russell, *op. cit.*, p. 165.

57 *Ibid.*, pp. 152-153.

58 *Ibid.*, p. 150.

59 *Ibid.*, p. 152.

60 *Vide*: C. D. Broad, "Berkeley's Argument against Material Substance", *Proceedings of the British Academy*, XXVIII, (1942).

61 B. Russell, *op. cit.*, p. 152.

62 Berkeley, *D.H.P.*, III, p. 313.

63 Berkeley, *Siris*, Section 289.

64 Berkeley, *D.H.P.*, III, p. 328.

65 Berkeley, *Commonplace Book*, in A. A. Luce and T. E. Jessop eds. *The Works of Berkeley*, I, 625: "Matter once allowed. I defy any man to prove that God is not matter."

66 Berkeley, *D.H.P.*, III, p. 339: "You [Hylas] talked often as if you thought I maintained the non-existence of Sensible Things. Whereas in truth no one can be more thoroughly assured of their existence than I am."

67 A. A. Luce, *The Dialectic of Immaterialism* (London, 1963), p. 127.

68 Because God is thought of as not only the cause of actual ideas of sense, but of *posse percipi* as well, John O. Wisdom describes Berkelcy's position as "Theocentric Phenomenalism". *Vide*: J. O. Wisdom, *The Unconscious Origin of Berkeley's Philosophy* (London, 1953), p. 21.

69 R. McRae, "Phenomenalism and Mill's Causation Theory", *Philosophy and Phenomenological Review*, IX (1948), 237.

70 Berkeley, *Principles* . . . , Section 59.

71 Berkeley, *D.H.P.*, III, pp. 310-311.

72 Paul Marhenke, "Phenomenalism", in *Philosophical Analysis*, ed. Max Black (Englewood Cliffs, New Jersey, 1963), pp. 281-282.

73 R. J. Hirst has said that "there are interesting anticipations of [linguistic phenomenalism] in Berkeley, though not in his official theory", *The Problems of Perception* (London, 1959), p. 76.

74 Berkeley, *Principles* . . . , Section 3.

75 D. W. Hamlyn, *Sensation and Perception* (New York, 1961), p. 107.

76 Berkeley, *D.H.P.*, I, pp. 266-267.

77 Berkeley, *T.V.V.E.*, Section 9: " . . . besides things . . . immediately perceived by any sense, there [are] other things suggested to the mind by means of those . . . immediate objects; which things so suggested are not objects of that sense, being in truth only objects of the imagination".

78 Rudolf Carnap, *The Logical Syntax of Language* (New York, 1937), p. 285.

79 Paul Marhenke, *op. cit.*, p. 282.

80 Berkeley, *Principles* . . . , Section 49.

81 Berkeley, *D.H.P.*, III, pp. 299-300: "Wood, stones . . . and the like things, which I name . . . are things that I know. And I should not have known them but that I perceived . . . ideas".

82 G. J. Warnock, *Berkeley*, p. 133.

83 Berkeley, *D.H.P.*, I, p. 241ff.

84 Berkeley, *Philosophical Commentaries*, No. 405, in *The Works of George Berkeley*, I.

85 Berkeley, *op. cit.*, No. 740.

86 A. A. Luce, *The Dialectic of Immaterialism*, p. 108.

87 Paul Marhenke, *op. cit.*, p. 281.

88 Applying Carnap's description of material modes of speech in his *The Logical Syntax of Language* to some of Berkeley's expressions we might detect some similarities. For, Berkeley does say that "Things are collections of ideas." And Carnap identifies the statement, "A thing is a complex of sense-data", as an illustration of a material mode of speech (p. 301). We could take Berkeley to mean that the word "thing" is to be used as synonymous with the phrase "collection of ideas". Hence, we might believe that Berkeley had anticipated the technique of using material modes of speech. This seems to be the case when he states that the word "die" is a symbol for "collection of ideas". But he also wants to say that the phrase "collection of ideas" refers to some actual experience or event occurring in consciousness (for, the colligation of sense-ideas is a mental act distinct from perception). To that extent, his statement is intended to have empirical reference and is, hence, not a proper use of the material mode of speech. In addition, Berkeley does seem to be concerned with what Carnap would call a pseudo-question (i.e., what a thing is). Berkeley was surely concerned with "what is the case" or with linguistic descriptions of the perceptual process. Therefore, his occasional use of what can anachronistically be called material modes of speech is accidental and the description of some of his central theses in these terms leads to a misunderstanding of HIS philosophical claims despite what Carnap (for example) might make of these truth-claims. Berkeley's occasional formalistic approaches to a discussion of perception are negated by his obvious metaphysical and empirical claims.

89 P. Marhenke, *loc. cit.*

90 Berkeley, *D.H.P.*, III, p. 340.

91 D. M. Armstrong, *Perception and the Physical World*, p. 54. *Cp.* I. Berlin, "Empirical Propositions and Hypothetical Statements", *Mind*, LIX.

92 *Vide*: Rudolf Carnap, *Der Logische Aufbau der Welt* (Berlin, 1928).

93 Alfred J. Ayer, *Language, Truth and Logic* (New York, n.d.), p. 63.

94 *Ibid.*

95 G. A. Johnston, *The Development of Berkeley's Philosophy* (London, 1923), p. 158: " . . . the thing that we perceive is *not* [according to Berkeley] immediately given in sensory experience, but is a *construct*".

96 Berkeley, *D.H.P.*, III, p. 319.

97 A. A. Luce has recently emphasized the importance of imagination in Berkeley's thought and has said that "... the term *exist* is usually confined to actual perception, but . . . Berkeley applies it, too, to imagined existence". *The Dialectic of Immaterialism*, p. 95.

98 Berkeley, *D.H.P.*, III, p. 328.

99 *Ibid.*, pp. 305-306.

V

Concluding Remarks

The basic intention of this interpretation has been to examine critically the nature of perception as it was conceived of by Berkeley, to trace the thread of consistency in his various arguments and, occasionally, to point to certain inconsistencies in the various aspects of his theory of perception. In addition to the attempt to draw out the implications of many of Berkeley's basic concepts and conclusions, an endeavor has been made to show explicitly what the relationship between Berkeley's perceptual theory and contemporary phenomenalism is. Although this relationship has often been stated, it has rarely been clearly explicated.

Although Berkeley's importance in the history of philosophy is obvious and well-known, the value of his analysis of perception has at times been obscured by criticisms which have been either too facile or based upon misconceptions of his essential position. Berkeley's perceptual theory has an additional importance because of the relationship which exists between that theory and contemporary phenomenalism and the phenomenalistic approaches often adopted in the philosophy of science. Although the recent attempts to make Berkeley a harbinger of the notion that the analysis of language is the only proper philosophical method are admittedly supported by SOME aspects of Berkeley's philosophical thought, it has been maintained that the metaphysical core of Berkeley's philosophy ultimately puts him outside the realm of linguistic analysis. Berkeley's phenomenalism is, if anything, a species of factual phenomenalism, not linguistic phenomenalism.

In the previous chapters it has been argued that Berkeley's analysis of perception ultimately leads him to phenomenalistic conclusions. It has been shown that perception, for Berkeley, is a passive, receptive process by which man is able to apprehend a system of appearances which enables him to operate efficiently in the various functions necessary for his existence. This pragmatic emphasis is one which is not absent from Berkeley's writings and, in a sense, may be said to be the primary value and significance of sense-perception. Thus, for example, in the *Essay towards a New Theory of Vision* Berkeley writes that

> the proper objects of Vision constitute the Universal Language of Nature; whereby we are instructed how to regulate our actions, in order to attain those things that are necessary to the preservation and well-being of our bodies . . . It is by their information that we are principally guided in all the transactions and concerns of life.[1]

The notion of the practical utility of sense-perception is one which Berkeley maintained throughout his discussion of perception. However, his descriptions of perception and his interpretation of the fundamental nature of perception, are sometimes ambiguous. As we have seen, he often tends to treat perception as if it included imagining, conceiving, willing, and inferring. He also tends to assert that perception is a mode of cognition even if it is, as he explicitly says in the *Siris*, an inferior mode of cognition. His contention seems to be that sense-perception provides us with that minimum amount of "knowledge" which is sufficient for the preservation of our existence. But perception involves the apprehension of appearances only, a multiplicity of phenomena which are fleeting, impermanent manifestations caused by the divine will. It may be said that if man were incapable of notional or intuitive knowledge, if, that is, human "knowledge" was derived exclusively from sense-perception, then man would indeed be in the condition of the chained men in Plato's cave. In this sense, it may be said – if our interpretation of Berkeley's perceptual theory is reasonably correct – that Berkeley's position may be described as a form of what may be called experiential phenomenalism. The use of this phrase distinguishes Berkeley's position from the Kantian and Neo-Kantian forms of phenomenalism which restrict human

KNOWLEDGE to phenomena alone. Berkeley tends to restrict sense-perception to the apprehension of phenomena, but insists that human knowledge can and does transcend this phenomenal mode of primitive cognition. Human knowledge, for Berkeley, seems to be the capacity by virtue of which a hierarchy of existents is apprehended. This hierarchy extends from the relative, dependent existents apprehended in sense-perception to the absolute existent, the divine mind. It may be said that Berkeley was a perceptual phenomenalist. If this is so, why is it so? This can be answered by summarizing some of his fundamental assertions.

At the conclusion of his analysis of the theory of vision Berkeley emphasized the following points: visual perception is the apprehension of a two-dimensional manifold of appearances; the ideas of touch and ideas of sight are heterogeneous; mediate perception (which is closely related to the process of suggestion) enables the perceiver to anticipate possible perceptions; tactile perception involves the apprehension of that which exists independent of the perceiver. Except for the last point – which was asserted for dialectical purposes – Berkeley consistently and repeatedly argued in defense of these notions. With the elimination of the "objective" character of tactile data in the *Principles* Berkeley then put forward his basic perceptual notion: that the various modalities of sense enable a perceiver to apprehend sense-data which are mind-dependent insofar as they cannot be said to exist without being in relation to a percipient being. It is believed that Berkeley has presented, *mutatis mutandis*, a relatively consistent defense of this fundamental conception. The consistency of his arguments in support of the mind-dependent nature of all sensory data depends, to be sure, on his somewhat ambiguous use of the term "idea". Berkeley uses the term idea to refer to (a) an object of thought; (b) a sense-quality; (c) a sensation; and (d) an image. Although we may criticize Berkeley for using a term to refer to so many various aspects of human experience, it is believed that Berkeley has used this term (as he defined it) more or less consistently and may be said to have tried to capitalize on the ambiguous character of the conception of "idea". It has been argued that Berkeley did not confuse the distinction between sensible qualities and sensations but was – as his analysis of primary and secondary qualities in the *Principles* and his analysis of the sensation of pain in the *Three Dialogues between Hylas and Philonous* indicates – quite aware of the distinction between sensations and sensible qualities. However, he argued that there is one thing that sensations and sense-qualities have (phenomenologically) in common and that is a relationship to a percipient being. He argues that the structure of the so-called qualities OF things seems to depend upon the position and condition of the percipient being. When Berkeley occasionally talks about qualities OF things we cannot assume that this is what he intends to say. For, he cautions us to

> Remember . . . that it is not any object which is hard or soft, hot or cold, blue or white, round or square, &c. For all these things I affirm do exist. Though . . . I deny they have an existence distinct from being perceived; or that they exist out of all minds whatsoever.[2]

To assert that sense-qualities, if they are said to exist only when they are perceived by finite minds or are known by God, can exist independent of all minds is, according to Berkeley, a contradiction in terms. For, sensory experience is possible only for a conscious reflective being who can attend to WHAT is experienced.

A basic contention of my interpretation of Berkeley's theory of perception is that he occasionally tends to incorporate aspects of the representational theory of perception, which he had attacked so vehemently, into his own theory. It has been argued that the sense-ideas apprehended by finite minds cannot be said to be identical to the ideas in the divine mind. The distinction Berkeley makes between ectypal or natural sense-phenomena and the archetypal "ideas" in the divine mind is one to which the internal structure of his perceptual theory led him. It is believed that Berkeley introduced this distinction for the following reasons. First, the sense-data apprehended by finite percipients are impermanent and fleeting, following one after the other in temporal succession. Second, the various congeries of sense-ideas apprehended by a multiplicity of percipients are similar and not identical. Berkeley could not consistently maintain that the temporal succession of sense-data is identical with what is "in the mind" of a supratemporal being. His theocentric phenomenalism (if such it may be called) undermines the claim that he is a common-sense realist and causes him to embrace a form of representationalism, a theory of perception he had repudiated. For, the sensory data apprehended by finite perceivers may be said to REPRESENT or copy the divine ideas. In addition, the divine, transcendent ideas are introduced in order to resolve the problem of identity. The eternal objects in the divine mind must ultimately be the REAL entities which the multiplicity of sense-data apprehended by finite percipients represent. Since Berkeley has insisted that he does not agree with the Malebranchean notion that we have access to the ideas in the divine mind, it appears that he has introduced an inaccessible element into his perceptual theory, the paradigmatic objects known by God. In addition, it may be argued that the things or phenomenal objects (which, it is believed, are "constructed" by the colligation of sense-ideas) formed by finite minds also may be said to represent the entities known by God. Sense-ideas must be thought of in some way as representing the divine ideas since the mode of existence of what is perceived by finite beings is relative and temporal and is completely other than the absolute, eternal existence of the things known by a divine intelligence. Ultimately, then, it may be said that Berkeley has, in a sense, introduced a marked representationalist element into his perceptual analyses, an element which his own criticisms of representationalism seem to undermine.

At any rate, it may be said that the phenomena apprehended in sense-perception are not ultimately real, but may be conceived of as appearances caused by the divine will which are contrasted with the transcendental reality of the eternal, immutable ideas or objects known by God. In this sense also Berkeley's position is phenomenalistic, though for different reasons.

There is another way in which, as we have seen, Berkeley tends to introduce representationalist notions into his perceptual theory. That is, his conception of mediate perception may be said to be a form of representationalism.[3] Berkeley describes mediate perception as the process of inferring possible perceptions from immediate perceptions. In mediate perception one modality of sense "suggests to the mind" what data would be perceived by other modalities of sense. In his *Three Dialogues between Hylas and Philonous* Berkeley avers that

> we may . . . be said to perceive . . . things mediately by sense — that is, when, from a frequently perceived connexion, the immediate perception of ideas by one sense suggests to the mind others . . . belonging to another sense, which are wont to be connected with them.[4]

Thus, for example, when I perceive that collection of sense-data I have learned to identify as a billiard ball, the solidity and smoothness of what is identified as a billiard ball are not apprehended in visual perception. These "ideas" are suggested to the imagination by the color and shape apprehended in perception. Of course, the tactile sense-data which are anticipated depend upon memory of past perceptions of similar collections of sense-ideas and upon certain preconceptions we have about such congeries of sense-data. This notion of mediate perception is obviously a strong phenomenalistic element in Berkeley's analysis of perception.

At any rate, in the process of the anticipation of perceptions there is a sharp distinction made between immediate perception and mediate perception. Immediate perception is an uncritical, pre-judgmental sense-awareness and mediate perception involves the process of inferring what may be perceived from what is perceived and implies a judgment about what is immediately perceived. Now, as we have argued, it would seem that Berkeley has introduced a form of representationalism into this conception of mediate perception. For it may be said that the sense-ideas apprehended in visual perception have a representational function insofar as they are said to signify what other perceptions may be experienced. It is believed that the process of mediate perception, as described by Berkeley, involves the imaginative representation of possible perceptions. It cannot be said that the sense-data signified by that which is immediately perceived are IDEAS OF SENSE.

The "ideas" signified in mediate perception must be ideas of imagination. Now, Berkeley has so defined ideas of imagination that they must be thought of as having a representative function. As a matter of fact, the greater "portion" of the phenomenal object is, in a sense, represented in imagination. Since we do not immediately perceive all of the sense-data out of which a phenomenal object is "constructed", it may be assumed that the imaginative representation of sense-data plays a significant role in the Berkeleyan perceptual theory. If this attempt to draw out the implications of Berkeley's position is justified, then we also have a clue concerning the nature of the activity by which the various phenomena apprehended in sense-perception are colligated or "joined together" by the percipient being. It would appear that if it is by means of mediate perception that a greater portion of the sense-data out of which the phenomenal object is constructed is apprehended, and if the data signified in mediate perception are ideas of imagination, then it is by means of the intentional activity of the will that the synthetic, phenomenal object is "formed". That is, an "object" is an intentional construct.

Related to the phenomenalistic interpretation of Berkeley's perceptual analysis is the thesis – presented primarily in Chapter III – that THINGS are not the immediate data apprehended in sense-perception. As we have seen, Berkeley occasionally claims that sensible things are the objects apprehended in perception. Such a view, it has been argued, is one which contradicts other assertions which Berkeley makes and is incongruous with an essential aspect of his perceptual analysis.

It has been contended that it is elementary sense-data which are immediately perceived. Berkeley describes these phenomena as "real things" insofar as they are " . . . known by the understanding, and produced by the will of an infinite Spirit". A sensible thing is a combination of sensible qualities or sensations which are colligated "by the mind". Berkeley cannot assert that things are directly perceived since he has said that the term "thing" usually denotes something which exists external to consciousness. The basic objects of sense are sense-data which cannot be said to exist unperceived. The specific entity or thing (a cherry tree, or tulip) is not something other than a congeries of sense-ideas. For, the qualities of such entities are "known" in the sense that we are acquainted with them through perception. The phenomenal thing is FORMED through the conflation of the various data apprehended by the modalities of sense. As Berkeley puts it:

> men combine together several ideas, apprehended by divers senses, or by the same sense at different times, or in different circumstances, but observed, however, to have some connexion in nature . . . all which they refer to one name, and consider as one thing.[5]

Although Berkeley has not, as far as we have seen, explained precisely HOW the data derived from sense-perception are combined or "joined together", it has been contended that Berkeley has put forward a rudimentary form of constructionism. It has also been suggested that the synthetic process of bringing together the various sense-data – since it seems to imply, to some extent, imaginative representation – is an intentional act which is distinct from the passive receptivity of sense. The conception of a phenomenal thing involves the selective perceptual apprehension of the sense-data from a "family" of regularly interrelated sense-data which may be said to constitute a specific entity. Berkeley's theory of perception attempts to account for the multiplicity of appearances which are apprehended in perception. Out of the apparent colors, apparent sizes, and apparent shapes which are perceived the perceiver is able to "construct" a phenomenal object or thing which can be reduced to the sense-contents out of which it was constructed. The perceptually derived phenomenal object cannot ultimately be said to be the REAL thing. That this is the case is indicated by Berkeley's statement in the *Three Dialogues between Hylas and Philonous* that

> the real tree, existing without the mind, is truly known and comprehended by (that is *exists in*) the infinite mind of God.[6]

The above comments serve to emphasize the claim that Berkeley's perceptual theory is distinctly a form of empirical or experiential phenomenalism. Sense-perception is, as we have seen, an inferior mode of cognition. It is perhaps for this reason that Berkeley is able to say in the *Siris* that "strictly the sense knows nothing". Since sense-data apprehended by finite percipients cannot be said to be identical with the "ideas" which have an eternal, unchanging existence in the mind of God, they must ultimately be considered as not completely real. It is Berkeley's insistence that man is capable not only of passively receiving sense-impressions, but of attaining notional, intuitive, and reflective modes of knowing that prevents us from describing Berkeley's philosophical position as acosmism or nihilism.

In regard to our examination of the relationship between the Berkeleyan theory of perception and contemporary forms of phenomenalism it is believed that this relationship has been made explicit in the discussions in Chapter IV. It has been argued that Berkeley's phenomenalism must be distinguished from what has been called linguistic phenomenalism. That is, the relationship between Berkeley's analysis of perception and linguistic phenomenalism has been overstated. Although there are, to be sure, certain suggestions of such a form of phenomenalism in Berkeley's writings, these suggestions are often not followed through by Berkeley and may ultimately be said to conflict with the factual orientation of his phenomenalistic assertions. That is to say that Berkeley often speaks in terms of the actual constituents of the world of relative existents. Berkeley's analysis of perception is most closely related to that form of phenomenalism which is indebted to that analysis (i.e., factual or experiential phenomenalism). The emphasis upon possible perceptions, the notion that things are not the immediate data apprehended in perception, the idea that a phenomenal object can be reduced to immediately (or mediately) experienced congeries of sense-data, the tendency to conceive of perception as a process in which appearances are apprehended — all of these basic notions link Berkeley with that mode of phenomenalism which has been described as factual phenomenalism. Berkeley's general position is that the analysis of perception is not primarily a linguistic problem, but an attempt to account for the phenomena perceived in the clearest and most efficient manner. Berkeley does not attempt to explain away the phenomena, but to "save the phenomena". His emphasis is not upon the language of perception, but upon the nature of perception as it is concretely experienced by finite beings.

Berkeley's phenomenalistic analysis of perception is, it is believed, one of the permanent contributions of philosophical investigation. It is a contribution, however, which must be seen against a metaphysical background which should neither be ignored nor negated. The extent of his influence cannot be measured. His originality is found not only in his multi-faceted perceptual analyses or his theory of knowledge, but in his phenomenalistic analysis of scientific concepts in *De Motu*. The phenomenalistic approach adopted by some philosophers of science is already implicit in this work. In much of the contemporary writing on perception there are echoes of Berkeley's insights and critical analyses. Perhaps Berkeley has not said the last word on the problem of perception, but what he has said is worthy of serious attention. Against those who charge that Berkeley generated a number of pseudo-problems which contemporary philosophers must abolish, it may be said that Berkeley was aware of the complexity of the perceptual process as it is experienced and was concerned to provide an account of the facts of perception. That his phenomenological description of the process of perception "violates common-sense" is not an argument against Berkeley unless one is committed to the METAPHYSICS of common-sense or to the metaphysical belief that conventional linguistic forms "describe", "picture", or "reveal" what is "real" or what is the case. That Berkeley occasionally falls into confusion may not be due to a misuse of language, but to the complex nature of what he was trying to describe.

Notes

1 Berkeley, *E.N.T.V.*, Section 147.

2 Berkeley, *D.H.P.*, III, p. 340.

3 It is interesting to note that H. H. Price claims that a theory which involves the notion of collecting perceptual data, not only what is actually perceived but what may be perceived, and which claims that a "thing" is a group of sense-data (or ideas) is a "representative theory of perception". *Perception*, p. 22n.

4 Berkeley, *D.H.P.*, I, pp. 266-267.

5 *Ibid.*, III, p. 319.

6 *Ibid.*, III, pp. 305-306.

Selected Bibliography

Aaron, R. I., "A Catalogue of Berkeley's Library", *Mind*, XLI (1932), 465-475.

__________, "Locke and Berkeley's Commonplace Book", *Mind*, N.S., XL (1931).

Armstrong, A. C., "Bergson, Berkeley and Philosophical Intuition", *Philosophical Review* (1914).

__________, "The Development of Berkeley's Theism", *Archiv für Geschichte der Philosophie*, N.F., Band 25 (1920), 150-161.

Armstrong, D. M., *Berkeley's Theory of Vision* (Victoria, Australia, 1960).

__________, *Perception and the Physical World* (New York, 1961).

Austin, J. L., *Sense and Sensibilia* (London, 1962).

Ayer, A. J., *The Foundations of Empirical Knowledge* (London, 1940).

__________, *Language, Truth and Logic* (London, 1935).

__________, *Philosophical Essays* (London, 1954).

__________, *The Problem of Knowledge* (London, 1956).

Bailey, S., "A Letter to a Philosopher in Reply to Some Recent Attempts to Vindicate Berkeley's Theory of Vision . . . " (London, 1843).

Baladi, N., *La pensée religieuse de Berkeley et l'unité de sa philosophie* (Le Caire, 1945).

Balfour, A. J., *Essays and Addresses* (Edinburgh, 1893).

Baratono, A., "Giorgio Berkeley e l'idealismo gnoseologico", *Rivista di filosofia* (Genova, 1916).

Beardsely, M. C., "Berkeley on Abstract Ideas", *Mind*, LII (1943), 157-170.

Bender, F., *George Berkeley's Philosophy Re-examined* (Amsterdam, 1956).

Bergson, H., "L'intuition philosophique", *Revue de métaphysique et de morale*, année 19, 809-827.

Bradley, F. H., *Appearance and Reality* (Oxford, 1930).

Brett, G. S., "Bishop Berkeley", *Royal Society of Canada*, XXVII (1933), 109-117.

Broad, C. D., "Berkeley's Argument against Material Substance", *Proceedings of the British Academy*, XXVIII (1942), 1-22.

_________, *Mind and Its Place in Nature* (London, 1925).

_________, "Phenomenalism", *Proceedings of the Aristotelian Society* (1914/1915).

Calkins, M., ed., *Berkeley: Selections* (New York, 1929).

Calkins, M. W., *The Persistent Problems of Philosophy* (New York, 1925).

Carnap, R., *The Logical Syntax of Language* (New York, 1937).

__________, *Der Logische Aufbau der Welt* (Berlin, 1928).

Carrau, L., "La philosophie religieuse de Berkeley", *Revue Philosophique*, XXII (1886), 376.

Cassirer, E., "Berkeley's System; ein Beitrage zur Geschichte und Systematik des Idealismus", *Philosophische Arbeiten*, Band 8 (Giessen, 1914).

__________, *The Philosophy of the Enlightenment*, tr. E. C. A. Koelln and J. P. Pettegrove (Boston, 1955).

Chisholm, R. M., *Perceiving: A Philosophical Study* (Ithaca, N.Y.), 1957.

Croce, B., "L'immaterialismo del Berkeley", *La Critica* (Bari, 1909).

Datta, D. M., "The Objective Idealism of Berkeley", *The Monist*, XLIII (1933), 220-235.

Davis, J. W., "Berkeley's Doctrine of the Notion", *The Review of Metaphysics*, XII (1959), 378-389.

Day, J. P. de C., "George Berkeley, 1685-1753, Part I", *The Review of Metaphysics*, VI (1952), 83-113.

__________, "George Berkeley, 1685-1753, Part II", *The Review of Metaphysics*, VI (1952), 265-286.

__________, "George Berkeley, 1685-1753, Part III", *The Review of Metaphysics*, VI (1953), 447-469.

_________, "George Berkeley, 1685-1753, Pat IV", *The Review of Metaphysics*, VI (1953), 583-596.

Dewey, J., *Essays in Experimental Logic*, Chicago, 1916.

_________, "Phenomenalism", in James Baldwin, ed., *Dictionary of Philosophy and Psychology*, II (New York, 1902).

Elbert, J. A., "Berkeley's Conception of God from the Standpoint of Perception and Causation", *The New Scholasticism*, VIII (1934), 152-158.

Emmet, D. M., *The Nature of Metaphysical Thinking* (London, 1957).

Ewing, A. C., *Idealism, A Critical Survey* (London, 1934).

Fawcett, E. D., "From Berkeley to Hegel", *The Monist*, III, 41-81.

Fearn, J., "A Review of First Principles of Bishop Berkeley, Dr. Reid and Prof. Stewart", *The Pamphleteer*, III (1814), 345-359.

Feigl, H., "The Mind-Body Problem in the Development of Logical Empiricism", in *Readings in the Philosophy of Science* (New York, 1953).

Ferrier, J. F., "Berkeley's Idealism", *Blackwoods Magazine* (June, 1842).

Forde, P., "An Irish Idealist", *Ecclesiastical Review*, X, 375-385.

Fraser, A. C., *Berkeley and Spiritual Realism* (London, 1908).

Fritz, A. D., "Berkeley's Self — Its Origin in Malebranche", *Journal of the History of Ideas*, XV (1954), 554-572.

Furlong, E. J., "Berkeley and the 'Knot about Inverted Images'", *Australasian Journal of Philosophy*, XLI (December, 1963), 306-316.

Gelber, S., "Universal Language and the Sciences of Man in Berkeley's Philosophy", *Journal of the History of Ideas*, XIII (1952), 482-513.

"George Berkeley", *California University Publications in Philosophy*, XXIX (1957).

Goodman, N., *The Structure of Appearance* (Cambridge, Mass., 1951).

Graham, E. C., *Optics and Vision in the Background of the Metaphysics of Berkeley* (New York, 1929).

Grey, D., "The Solipsism of Bishop Berkeley", *The Philosophical Quarterly,* II (1952), 338-349.

Hamilton, W., *Lectures on Metaphysics and Logic*, I (Boston, 1867).

Hamlyn, D. W., *Sensation and Perception* (New York, 1961).

Hedenius, I., *Sensationalism and Theology in Berkeley's Philosophy* (Uppsala, 1936).

Hicks, G. D., *Berkeley* (London, 1932).

Hirst, R. J., *The Problem of Perception* (London, 1959).

Hoernlé, R. F. A., *Idealism as a Philosophy* (New York, 1927).

"Homage to George Berkeley", *Hermathena*, No. 82 (1953).

Hone, J. M., and M. M. Rossi, *Bishop Berkeley* (London, 1930).

Hume, D., *A Treatise of Human Nature* (New York, 1961).

Huxley, T. H., *Hume, with Helps to the Study of Berkeley* (New York, 1902).

Jessop, T. E., "The Influence of Malebranche on Berkeley", *Revue Internationale de Philosophie* (Bruxelles, 1938).

Jessop, T. E., and A. A. Luce, eds., *The Works of George Berkeley* (London, 1948), 9 Vols.

Johnston, G. A., "Berkeley's Logic of Mathematics", *Monist*, XXVIII (1918), 25-44.

_________, *The Development of Berkeley's Philosophy* (London, 1923).

_________, "The Relation between Collier and Berkeley", *Archiv für Geschichte der Philosophie*, Band 25 (1920), 162-175.

Johnston, S. P., "An Unpublished Essay by Berkeley on Infinities", *Hermathena*, Vol. II, No. 26, 180-185.

Joseph, H. W. B., *Essays in Ancient and Modern Philosophy* (London, 1935).

Joussain, A., *Exposé critique de la philosophie de Berkeley* (Paris, 1920).

Kant, I., *Critique of Pure Reason*, tr. M. Müller (London, 1907).

Kantonen, M., "The Influence of Descartes on Berkeley", *Philosophical Review* (1921).

Kaveeshwar, G. W., *The Metaphysics of Berkeley Critically Examined . . .* (Khandwa, 1933).

Körner, S., *Kant* (London, 1955).

Laird J., "Berkeley's Realism", *Mind*, XXI (1916), 308-328.

__________, *Hume's Philosophy of Human Nature* (London, 1932).

Lazerowitz, M., *The Structure of Metaphysics* (London, 1955).

Lean, M., *Sense-Perception and Matter* (London, 1953).

Lenin, V. I., *Materialism and Empirio-Criticism* (Moscow, 1952).

Leroux, E., "Note sur l'influence de Malebranche sur Berkeley", *Revue de Metaphysique et de morale* (Paris, 1938).

Lewis, C. I., *An Analysis of Knowledge and Valuation* (La Salle, Illinois, 1947).

__________, *Mind and the World Order* (New York, 1956).

Locke, J., *An Essay on the Human Understanding* (London, n.d.), 2 vols.

Loewy, T., "Der Idealismus Berkeley's im der Grundlagen Untersuchten", *Kais, Akad. der Wissenschaft*, Band 124 (Wein, 1891).

Luce, A. A., *Berkeley and Malebranche* (London, 1934).

__________, "The Berkeleian Idea of Sense", *Proceedings of the Aristotelian Society*, Supplementary Vol. XXVII (1953), 1-20.

__________, "Berkeley's Doctrine of the Perceivable", *Hermathena*, IX (1942), 3-15.

__________, "Berkeley's Existence in the Mind", *Mind*, L (1941), 258-267.

__________, *Berkeley's Immaterialism* (London, 1950).

__________, *Berkeley's Thought* (New York, 1934).

__________, *The Dialectic of Immaterialism* (London, 1964).

__________, *The Life of George Berkeley, Bishop of Cloyne* (London, 1949).

__________, *Sense without Matter* (London, 1954).

__________, "The Unity of the Berkeleian Philosophy", *Mind*, XLVI (1937), 44-52; 180-190.

Mabbot, J. D., "The Place of God in Berkeley's Philosophy", *Journal of Philosophic Studies* (London, 1931).

Mach, E., *The Analysis of Sensations*, tr. S. Waterlow (New York, 1959).

__________, *The Science of Mechanics: A Critical and Historical Account of Its Development*, tr. T. J. McCormack (Chicago, 1902).

Mahony, M., "George Berkeley: Irish Idealist", *Thought*, I (1926), 78-101.

Malcolm, N., "Direct Perception", *Philosophical Quarterly*, III (1953), 301-316.

March, W. W. S., "Analogy, Aquinas and Bishop Berkeley", *Theology*, XLIV (1942), 321-329.

Marhenke, P., "Phenomenalism", in M. Black (ed.), *Philosophical Analysis* (Ithaca, Cornell University Press, 1950).

McCosh, J., "Locke's Theory of Knowledge, with a Notice of Berkeley", *Philosophic Series*, No. 5, IV (1884).

Metz, R., *George Berkeley: Leben und Lehre* (Stuttgart, 1925).

Mill, J. S., "Bailey on Berkeley's Theory of Vision", in *Dissertations and Discussions*, II (London, n.d.).

__________, "Berkeley's Life and Writings", in *Dissertations and Discussions*, IV (London, n.d.).

__________, *An Examination of Sir William Hamilton's Philosophy* (New York, 1884).

__________, *A System of Logic* (London, 1843).

Montague, W. P., *Ways of Knowing* (New York, Macmillan, 1925).

Moore, G. E., *Philosophical Studies* (London, Routledge, Kegan Paul, Ltd., 1922).

__________, *Some Main Problems of Philosophy* (New York, Collier Books, 1962).

Morgan, L., "Notes on Berkeley's Doctrine of Esse", *Proceedings of the Aristotelian Society*, XV (1915), 100-139.

Morris, C. R., *Locke, Berkeley, Hume* (London, Oxford University Press, 1931).

Paget S., "The Influence of Berkeley", *Nineteenth Century and After*, LVIII (1905), 252-258.

Paul, L., *The English Philosophers* (London, 1952).

Pearson, K., *The Grammar of Science* (New York, Meridian Books, Inc., 1957).

Perry, R. B., *Present Philosophical Tendencies* (Longmans, Green and Co., 1912).

Pfeil, H., "Der psychologismus im englischen empirismus", *Forschungen zur neueren philosophie . . .* , V (1934).

Popkin, R. H., "Berkeley's Pyrrhonism", *The Review of Metaphysics*, V (1951), 223-246.

Prichard, H. A., "The Sense-Datum Fallacy", *Proceedings of the Aristotelian Society*, LVII (1938), 1-18.

Reid, T., *Essays on the Intellectual Powers of Man* (Edinburgh, 1941).

Richtie, A. D., "George Berkeley's *Siris*", *Proceedings of the British Academy*, XL (1954), 41-55.

Rolleston, T. W., "Two Makers of Modern Ireland", *Fortnightly Review*, XCI (1909), 1100-1116.

Rome, S. C., "Berkeley's Conceptualism", *Philosophical Review*, LV (1946), 680-686.

__________, "Scottish Refutation of Berkeley's Immaterialism", *Philosophy and Phenomenological Research*, III (1943), 313-325.

Russell, B., *The Analysis of Matter* (New York, 1954).

__________, *Human Knowledge: Its Scope and Limits* (New York, 1948).

__________, *Mysticism and Logic* (New York, 1957).

__________, *Our Knowledge of the External World* (London, 1926).

__________, *The Problems of Philosophy* (London, 1912).

Sartre, J. P., *Being and Nothingness*, tr. H. E. Barnes (New York, 1956).

Schlick, M., "Positivism and Realism", in *Logical Positivism*, ed. A. J. Ayer (Glencoe, Illinois, 1959).

Sellers, W., *Science, Perception and Reality* (New York, 1963).

Senden, M. von, *Space and Sight*, tr. P. Heath (Glencoe, Illinois, 1960).

Seth, J., *English Philosophers & Schools of Philosophy* (London, 1925).

Sillem, E. A., *George Berkeley and the Proofs for the Existence of God* (London, 1957).

Stace, W. T., *The Nature of the World* (Princeton, N.J., 1940).

__________, "The Refutation of Realism", *Mind*, LIII (1934).

__________, *Theory of Knowledge and Existence* (Oxford, 1932).

Stack, George J., "Berkeley's Concept of Objects", *Modern Schoolman* (November, 1967), 1-27.

__________, Review of Warren E. Steinkraus, ed., *New Studies in Berkeley's Philosophy, Journal of the History of Philosophy* (April, 1967), 178-180.

Steinkraus, W. E., ed., *New Studies in Berkeley's Philosophy* (New York, 1967).

Turbayne, C. M., "Berkeley and Molyneux on Retinal Images", *Journal of the History of Ideas* (June, 1955).

_________, "Berkeley's Two Concepts of Mind", *Philosophy and Phenomenological Research*, XX (1959), 85-92.

_________, "Berkeley's Two Concepts of Mind", *PPR*, XXIII (1962), 577-580.

Wallraff, C. F., "Sense-Datum Theory and Observational Fact", *The Journal of Philosophy*, LV (1958), 20-32.

Warnock, G. J., *Berkeley* (London, 1953).

Weyl, H., *Philosophy of Mathematics and Natural Science*, trans. O. Helmer (Princeton, 1949).

Wild, J., *George Berkeley* (London, 1936).

Wisdom J. O., "The Analyst Controversy: Berkeley as a Mathematician", *Hermathena*, LIX (1942), 111-128.

_________, "The Analyst Controversy: Berkeley's Influence on the Development of Mathematics", *Hermathena*, No. 54 (1939), 3-29.

_________, *The Unconscious Origin of Berkeley's Philosophy* (London, 1953).

Woodworth, R. S., and H. Schlosberg, *Experimental Psychology* (New York, 1956).

Index